A FIELD GUIDE ON
FALSE TEACHING

LIGONIER MINISTRIES

CONTENTS

INTRODUCTION

With just over 30 percent of the world's population professing to be Christians as of 2017, Christianity is the largest and most widespread religion in the world.[1] However, there exists an astonishingly wide diversity of opinions about doctrine and practice under the umbrella of Christianity.[2] While many professing Christians have an accurate understanding of the theology of Scripture, not all professing Christians understand the core biblical doctrines of the faith as summarized in the classic Christian creeds and confessions, and many of those who claim to follow Jesus hold beliefs that deny biblical teaching. Moreover, Christians must interact daily with people at work and in their communities who make no Christian profession and perhaps even challenge the Bible's teaching.

False teaching—both inside and outside the church—has always been proclaimed against the truth of Scripture. It is therefore essential that believers be well versed in the biblical doctrines of revelation, God, man, sin, Christ, atonement, salvation, and eternity. Believers should also seek to be conversant with the essential features of false teaching, religions, and worldviews so that they can recognize error and refute it for the sake of the gospel. To that end, this work is an introduction to current false teachings in the church and false religions in the world. It is not an exhaustive survey, but rather it seeks to point out many of the false teachings in our day. It is our sincere desire that this booklet will help you be better "prepared to make a defense to anyone who asks you for a reason for the hope that is in you" (1 Peter 3:15).

Essential Christian truths

Although everything God reveals in the Scriptures may be considered "essential" to the life of the church, some biblical doctrines are more important to the system of Christian truth than others. When considering false teaching and religions, the following biblical doctrines are vital to maintaining Christianity as it was given to us by Jesus and the Apostles.

Revelation

Theologians refer to God's revelation of Himself in creation and the human conscience as general revelation and to His revelation in Scripture as special revelation. General revelation discloses God's eternal power and divine nature as well as His basic moral law for humanity (Ps. 19:1–6; Rom. 1:18–2:16). Special revelation gives us God's fuller revelation of His character, His plan of salvation for mankind, and His instructions for living lives that please Him (Ps. 19:7–11; 2 Tim. 3:16–17). The Old and New Testaments are the full and final special revelation of God. With the sixty-six books of the Bible, God has given us "all things that pertain to life and godliness" (2 Peter 1:3). The Scriptures are infallible and inerrant. All that God has revealed in His Word is authoritative, sufficient, clear, and necessary for the salvation of believers, the lives of Christians, and the ministry of the church. The central message of Scripture is God's salvation in the person and work of Christ (Luke 24:27, 44).

There is no other special revelation from God after the close of the canon of Scripture.

God

The starting place of all truth is the holy God Himself. When we look into Scripture, we discover that the one true and living God is infinite (1 Kings 8:27; Ps. 147:5), eternal (Ps. 90:1; Isa. 57:15), and unchangeable (Mal. 3:6) in all His divine perfections (Ex. 34:6; Num. 14:18; Neh. 9:31; Ps. 86:5, 15; Joel 2:13). Within the one Godhead there subsist three persons—Father, Son, and Holy Spirit. These three persons are the one true and living God. The Father, Son, and Spirit are the same in substance and equal in power and glory. God is the Holy Trinity.

Man

At creation, God made humanity male and female, in His own image, in knowledge, righteousness, and holiness (Gen. 1:26–27; Eph. 4:24; Col. 3:10). God commissioned men and women to fill the earth and have dominion over it (Gen. 1:28). He entered into a covenant of works with Adam at creation, forbidding him to eat of the Tree of Knowledge of Good and Evil, promising life upon obedience and death upon disobedience (Gen. 2:15–17; Rom. 5:12–21). This prohibition to eat of the Tree of Knowledge of Good and Evil was meant both to test Adam's obedience and to remind him that God is the Creator and man the creature.

Sin

When Adam disobeyed God and ate of the Tree of Knowledge of Good and Evil, he fell from the condition in which God originally made him. By his disobedience, Adam brought sin and death into the world. Adam stood as the representative of all his descendants, so that everyone who descends from him by natural generation sinned in him and fell with him (Rom. 5:12–21; 1 Cor. 15:22). Adam's natural-born descendants have had his guilt imputed to them, have been deprived of the original righteousness that Adam possessed, and have had the corruption of his nature passed on to them. By nature, all people (except Christ) are "dead in . . . trespasses and sins" and under the wrath and curse of God (Eph. 2:1–3). Actual sins that we commit proceed from the corruption of our nature and are transgressions of the law of God or failures to keep His law. As the Apostle John wrote, "Sin is lawlessness" (1 John 3:4).

Christ

The Lord Jesus Christ, the eternal Son of God and second person of the Trinity, became incarnate in the fullness of time, adding a human nature to Himself and thus uniting Himself to our humanity. Jesus is truly God and truly man in one person forever. Jesus is the only Mediator between God and man. He lived a sinless life in order to fulfill the demands of the law of God (Rom. 5:12–21; Gal. 4:3–4), and He laid down His life as an atoning sacrifice for His sheep (John 10:15). In His death, Jesus propitiated—satisfied and turned away—the wrath of God by taking the punishment for the sins of His people. Jesus rose from the dead on the third day. He ascended to heaven, where He is seated "at the right hand of the Majesty on high" (Heb. 1:3). Jesus will come again in glory to consummate all things and judge the living and the dead. His rule as King of the kingdom of God will never end.

Salvation

Salvation is by grace alone through faith alone in Christ alone to the glory of God alone. God chose a people for Himself in His Son before the foundation of the world (Eph. 1:3–4). The Son lived and died to atone for the sins of those whom God has chosen (John 10:29). The salvation that Christ accomplished by His death and resurrection is applied to His people by the Holy Spirit of God, the third person of the Godhead. The Holy Spirit regenerates those for whom Christ died, bringing them from death to life (John 3:5). All those who are born again by the Spirit of God come to trust in Christ and are united to Him by faith alone. When a sinner is united to Christ by faith, he is justified, set apart, and adopted as a child of God. Everyone who is united to Christ will be glorified when he dies or when Christ comes again on the last day.

Eternity

The Bible teaches that there is a final day of judgment on which all people will stand before the throne of God and will have to give an account of everything they have done in the body (Rom. 14:12; 2 Cor. 5:10). The spirits of believers who die before that final day will go to be with Christ in heaven, whereas the spirits of those who have not trusted in Christ and who die before that final day will suffer in hell (Mark 9:45; Luke 12:5; 16:19–31; 2 Cor. 5:8; Phil. 1:23). The bodies of both believers and unbelievers who die before the final day of judgment will remain in the grave, awaiting the final bodily resurrection on judgment day (Acts 24:15). On the last day, when Christ returns, all those who have died before His coming will be raised. All those who have trusted in Christ will receive glorified bodies, united to their spirits, and will go to be with Him in glory forever, dwelling with Him in the new heaven and earth. Everyone who has not trusted in Jesus alone for salvation will perish eternally in the lake of fire (John 3:36; 1 Cor. 15:35–57; Rev. 20–21).

BEING PREPARED TO MAKE A DEFENSE

Defending the faith

God instructs believers to always be "prepared to make a defense [Greek *apologia*] to anyone who asks you for a reason for the hope that is in you" (1 Peter 3:15). Apologetics involves giving people a well-reasoned statement or defense; it is a verbal and rational defense of the Christian faith. In order for us to give an effective defense of the truth, we first and foremost must be well versed in Scripture. Defending the truth of God's Word against falsehoods and lies is an integral part of the Christian's life and service. To do so effectively, we must also be prepared to defend the truth against false teachings and practices that run counter to the truth of Scripture.

In addition to giving a verbal reasoned defense of the truth of Scripture, Christians are to give a defense of the truth in the way we live and act. The Christian's witness to the truth often comes in response to the world's observation of how the faith is worked out in the Christian's life. Peter introduced an ethical dimension to the command to defend the faith. He exhorted believers to give a defense "with gentleness and respect" (1 Peter 3:15). Our lives serve as a defense of the truth. Jesus taught His disciples, "By this all people will know that you are my disciples, if you have love for one another" (John 13:35). The Apostle Paul charged believers to commit to "speaking the truth in love" (Eph. 4:15). This is a key element of defending the faith. The manner in which we speak the truth is a vital aspect of our defense of the truth. This is important both for pastors and for laypeople. As the Apostle Paul wrote Timothy, "The Lord's servant must not be quarrelsome but kind to everyone, able to teach . . . correcting his opponents with gentleness" (2 Tim. 2:24).

Contending for the faith

In addition to being called to defend the faith, Christians are to proactively "contend for the faith" (Jude 3). The church is to be proactive in the advancement of the truth of the Christian faith by exposing, refuting, rebuking, and correcting theological error (Eph. 5:11; 2 Tim. 2:25; Titus 1:13; 2:15). This is seen in the way that Paul interacted with the false teachings and ideologies represented in Athens (Acts 17:16–34). Ministers especially are given a responsibility to contend for the truth on behalf of the members of the church. This includes exposing false teaching and false living that contradict the truth. Paul instructs Titus to rebuke those whose lives contradict the gospel so "that they may be sound in the faith" (Titus 1:13). He also referred to those who "profess to know God, but they deny him by their works" (v. 16). The Apostle John charged the church not to give someone an opportunity to spread false teaching among the Christian community (2 John 9–11). Paul charged the elders in Ephesus to be alert to the fact that men would arise from among them "speaking twisted things, to draw away the disciples after them" (Acts 20:30). This call to contend for the faith is a common theme in the Pastoral Epistles (1 Tim. 1:3–4; 2 Tim. 1:13; Titus 3:9).

Proclaiming the faith

Inasmuch as God has appointed pastors to guard the truth (2 Tim. 1:14), the preaching of the Word of God is the primary means of the defense and preservation of the truth. God has instituted the preaching of the gospel as the central means by which He advances His kingdom (Rom. 10:14–17; 1 Cor. 1:21). The preaching of the Word is also the central means of correcting error and false teaching. Paul charged Timothy: "Preach the word; be ready in season and out of season; reprove, rebuke, and exhort, with complete patience and teaching. For the time is coming when people will not endure sound teaching, but having itching ears they will accumulate for themselves teachers to suit their own passions, and will turn away from listening to the truth and wander off into myths" (2 Tim. 4:2–4).

Though not all are called and gifted to preach and teach in the church, all the members of the church are called

"

IN YOUR HEARTS
HONOR CHRIST
THE LORD AS HOLY,
ALWAYS BEING
PREPARED TO MAKE
A DEFENSE TO
ANYONE WHO ASKS
YOU FOR A REASON
FOR THE HOPE
THAT IS IN YOU.

1 PETER 3:15

by God to be faithful in the propagation of His Word in their daily interactions with others. As Paul commended the members of the church in Thessalonica, "For not only has the word of the Lord sounded forth from you . . . but your faith in God has gone forth everywhere" (1 Thess. 1:8). As ministers faithfully proclaim the truth of God's Word, believers will be better equipped to faithfully carry the truth of Scripture out into their everyday relationships. To that end, it is our hope that each section of this work will serve as an aid to both pastors and congregants who desire to be faithful in their defense and proclamation of the Christian faith.

I.

FALSE
TEACHING

INTRODUCTION TO

FALSE
TEACHING

The refutation of false teaching in the church formed a significant part of the teaching ministry of the Old Testament prophets, the Lord Jesus Christ, and the Apostles. In fact, many of the New Testament writings were written specifically to combat the threat of false teaching and controversy in the early church.

Jesus and the Apostles constantly battled legalistic perversions of the doctrine of justification by faith alone (Luke 18:9–14; Rom. 4:1–12; 10:1–13; Gal. 2:16–21; 3:1–14), counterfeit prophecies (Matt. 7:15; Acts 20:30; 1 Thess. 5:20–21; 2 Peter 2:1; 1 John 4:1–3), aberrant views of the resurrection (Mark 12:18–27; 1 Cor. 15), rejections of the deity of Christ (John 10:33; 1 John 2:22–23; 2 John 9–10), denials of Jesus' second coming (1 Thess. 4:13–18; 2 Peter 3:4), and dismissive lawlessness (Matt. 7:21–23; 1 Cor. 6:12–20; 1 John 5; Jude 4). From start to finish, the New Testament addresses doctrinal controversy and refutes error.

Just as the church during the Apostolic age was buffeted by various false teachings, the church today continues to be threatened by a number of false doctrines. Prosperity gospels, the rejection of God's sovereignty and providence, denials of the deity of Christ, legalistic teaching on justification and sanctification, and antinomianism (i.e., lawlessness) are some of the false teachings that have taken root in various churches today. Ministers and congregants alike must stand against these forms of false teaching whenever and wherever they surface. In this section, we will summarize the history, key figures, and essential beliefs of several false teachings that threaten the modern church. Additionally, we will compare the essential beliefs of these systems of false teaching with biblical teaching. Finally, we will offer some practical considerations for how we can effectively share the gospel with those who have embraced these false teachings. It is our desire that this will help equip you to better "contend for the faith that was once for all delivered to the saints" (Jude 3) and to more faithfully witness to the grace of God in the gospel of our Lord Jesus Christ.

THE PROSPERITY GOSPEL

What is the prosperity gospel?

The prosperity gospel is one of the most prominent false teaching movements of our day. Prosperity gospel preachers and televangelists have deceived multitudes around the world with a false gospel, teaching that individuals who exercise true faith in Christ will surely attain physical, material, and financial prosperity in this life.

When did it begin?

The Apostolic church had its fair share of false teachers who perverted the truth of the gospel by turning it into a tool for monetary profit or into a way to manipulate God for power (Acts 8:9–24; 19:11–20). Throughout church history, there have been many forms of this sort of false teaching. The modern-day prosperity gospel movement began in the 1950s as a post–World War II Pentecostal movement through the ministry of Oral Roberts, an American televangelist. Roberts' books helped disseminate the message of the prosperity gospel movement. *If You Need Healing Do These Things* and *The Miracle of Seed-Faith* were among Roberts' more popular works. The movement was carried forward by Jim Bakker and Jimmy Swaggart, both of whom led massively influential televangelist ministries in the 1980s. Other key figures in the history of the movement include E.W. Kenyon and Kenneth E. Hagin.

Who are the key figures?

Kenneth Copeland, Benny Hinn, Joel Osteen, T.D. Jakes, John Hagee, Creflo Dollar, Paula White, Joyce Meyer, and Juanita Bynum are a few of the leading televangelists who have commercialized the teaching of the prosperity

"

I KNOW HOW TO
BE BROUGHT LOW,
AND I KNOW HOW
TO ABOUND. IN
ANY AND EVERY
CIRCUMSTANCE,
I HAVE LEARNED
THE SECRET OF
FACING PLENTY AND
HUNGER, ABUNDANCE
AND NEED.

PHILIPPIANS 4:12

gospel in our day. For decades, these men and women have broadcast a false gospel over the radio and on television channels such as the Trinity Broadcast Network (TBN). In this way, they have exported their false teaching to Africa, South America, and Asia as well.

What are the main beliefs?

The prosperity gospel movement has four main beliefs:

I. **Jesus purchased all the benefits of salvation for this life.** Jesus purchased complete physical healing for His people in this life through His death on the cross. By perverting the teaching of Isaiah 53:5 and John 10:10, prosperity gospel preachers assert that Jesus died to take away every sickness in this life and to atone for the "sin" of financial poverty.

II. **A present-day inheritance.** In the Abrahamic covenant, God promised a vast material and financial inheritance for believers in this life. If a person believes in Jesus, he will inherit great possessions and tangible blessings in this life.

III. **Give to get.** Prosperity gospel preachers teach their followers that the way to gain riches is to give more money to the kingdom, especially by giving to their churches and ministries. The quantity of material and financial prosperity one expects to gain is in proportion to what one gives.

IV. **Name it and claim it.** Faith and prayer empower people to lay hold of physical and material blessings in this life. Certain leaders in this movement have popularized the term *Word of Faith* to capture the essence of their teaching. Accordingly, if someone exercises enough faith, he will no longer have to be subject to the crippling effects of sickness and disease. If individuals continue to suffer afflictions or poverty, it is due to their lack of personal faith. When we pray in faith, we compel God to make us prosperous, particularly when we declare that we already possess the desired blessing. Likewise, some teachers discourage their followers from speaking negative words, lest they bring negative things into being.

Why do people believe this form of false teaching?

The false teachers of the prosperity gospel target their hearers' desires for provision, position, and power. Instead of focusing on Christ, eternity, and the glory of God, they place an emphasis on living one's "best life now." Many people in economically depressed communities and in Third World countries follow this teaching because it holds out promises of social empowerment and deliverance from extreme poverty and disease. Others follow the teaching because it justifies greed.

How does it hold up against biblical Christianity?

According to Scripture, physical, material, and financial prosperity are no sure marks of God's favor, and suffering is no sure mark of His displeasure. The Bible teaches that material prosperity is often a snare (Luke 12:15) and that suffering is often a mark of blessing (Matt. 5:10; 1 Peter 3:14). God's Word teaches neither that the Christian life is *all* physical and material prosperity, nor that it is *all* suffering. Rather, it teaches that there may be times of prosperity and times of suffering in the believer's life (Phil. 4:12). Scripture warns us not to set our hearts on riches (Ps. 62:10), and it teaches wealthy believers not to trust in their wealth (1 Tim. 6:17).

In contrast to the four main beliefs of the prosperity gospel, Scripture teaches the following:

I. In the Apostolic preaching of the cross, God calls people to come to Christ for the forgiveness of sins. Jesus died to atone for the sins of His people (Acts 2:38; 5:31; 10:43; 13:38; 26:18). The focus is never on physical, financial, or material prosperity in this life. While Jesus does secure everlasting blessings—including physical healing—for His people through His death on the cross, believers will come to enjoy the full benefits of the death of Christ only in the resurrection on the last day.

II. God promised Abraham that he would inherit the world (Rom. 4:13). This promise was fulfilled in the person and work of the Son of Abraham, Jesus Christ

(Gal. 3:16). Everyone who believes in Jesus Christ is a son or daughter of Abraham and coheir of the inheritance promised to him (Gal. 3:29). By the same faith Abraham exercised, we receive the blessings of salvation—justification, adoption, the promised Holy Spirit, and the guarantee of the everlasting inheritance (Gal. 3:7–9). Believers will not fully possess the inheritance until the resurrection on the last day (Heb. 11:39–40; 13:14).

III. Believers have the duty and privilege of giving generously to the work of God's kingdom in this life. God makes His grace abound toward His people when they give generously so that they will be equipped to continue giving generously (2 Cor. 9:8–11). Scripture never teaches us to give in order to gain and lay up treasure for ourselves.

IV. The Apostle Paul prayed fervently to the Lord for personal healing, only to have Jesus tell him, "My grace is sufficient for you, for my power is made perfect in weakness" (2 Cor. 12:7–9). This was not a lack of faith on Paul's part. God has not promised complete healing in this life. He promises complete healing for individuals only in the resurrection on the last day.

How can I share the gospel with those who hold to this false teaching?

I. **Focus on Christ's life and death for the forgiveness of sins.** The central message of the gospel is that Jesus Christ died for the sins of His people. Jesus shed His blood on the cross in order to cover the sin of those for whom He died. The gospel reconciles sinners to God through the person and work of Christ. The Apostle Paul explained the message of the cross when he wrote, "For our sake he made him to be sin who knew no sin, so that in him we might become the righteousness of God" (2 Cor. 5:21) and "Christ redeemed us from the curse of the law by becoming a curse for us—for it is written, 'Cursed is everyone who is hanged on a tree'—so that in Christ Jesus the blessing of Abraham might come to the Gentiles, so that we might receive the promised Spirit through faith" (Gal. 3:13–14).

II. **Focus on the hope of eternal blessing.** The Bible encourages believers to hope in God and to look forward to the eternal inheritance He has reserved for us. The Apostle Peter encouraged suffering believers to remember that they are being preserved by God for "an inheritance that is imperishable, undefiled, and unfading, kept in heaven for you" (1 Peter 1:4). The writer of Hebrews also taught, "Here we have no lasting city, but we seek the city that is to come" (Heb. 13:14). The Apostle Paul explained that the sufferings we endure in this life are prerequisites to obtaining the eternal inheritance: "The Spirit himself bears witness with our spirit that we are children of God, and if children, then heirs—heirs of God and fellow heirs with Christ, provided we suffer with him in order that we may also be glorified with him" (Rom. 8:16–17).

III. **Focus on the comfort we receive from sharing in Christ's sufferings.** Suffering is everywhere presented in Scripture as a prerequisite to glory (Rom. 8:17). Jesus was Himself a "man of sorrows and acquainted with grief" (Isa. 53:3). His was a life of reproach, hardship, difficulty, opposition, poverty, loneliness, and suffering (Luke 9:58). His disciples followed in His footsteps. The only one of Jesus' disciples to fall away was himself a lover of money (John 12:6). God has ordained that His people will suffer for the sake of Christ in this life (Phil. 1:29). He has promised resurrection wholeness, restoration, and abundance in the world to come (Rev. 21:4).

—

WORD OF FAITH

Word of Faith is a worldwide evangelical Christian movement that teaches that human beings have the power to bring things into being through the power of speech. Often associated with the Pentecostal and charismatic movements, Word of Faith holds that people, by virtue of being created in the image of God, are themselves creators and can carry out creative acts through their words just as God did in creation. Adherents are thus encouraged to speak positive words about their circumstances. Conversely, they are urged never to speak negative words, for doing so can bring those things into being. E.W. Kenyon is often cited as the originator of this teaching, and Kenneth Hagin Sr. was a prominent proponent.

ORAL ROBERTS

► 1918–2009

Oral Roberts was an American Pentecostal and charismatic evangelist, revivalist, and faith healer. He was a pioneer in the theology of seed-faith and in televangelism, having begun preaching on the radio in 1947 and on TV in 1954. After reading 3 John 2—"I wish above all things that thou mayest prosper and be in health, even as thy soul prospereth" (KJV)—he concluded that Christians may be wealthy. He founded the Oral Roberts Evangelistic Association and Oral Roberts University, along with a medical school and hospital, where modern medicine was combined with biblical healing principles.

DEISM

What is deism?

Deism is a religious philosophy that flourished in the eighteenth and nineteenth centuries, but its effects linger into our present age. Deism teaches that all people can know and believe in a Supreme Being—the prime mover of all things—merely through the vehicle of reason. Historically, deists often held to a modified form of Christianity that emptied the faith of any supernatural elements while allowing its moral instruction to remain. Though it is more of a philosophical and religious set of ideals than an organized religion, deism offers an antisupernatural worldview as an alternative to Christian theism.

When did it begin?

Although many of the principles of deism stem from the philosophical musings of early philosophers, it was not until the time of Edward Herbert, Lord Herbert of Cherbury (1583–1648)—the father of English deism—that it became a formulated alternative to biblical Christianity. Herbert was heavily influenced by the writings of medieval scholastics on natural religion. In his influential work *De Religione Gentilium* (Pagan religion), Herbert argued that it is immoral to insist that pagan nations—which have not had access to Scripture—deserve to be punished by God. Herbert developed the principle of deism out of a desire to rescue from eternal punishment those who had never been exposed to biblical revelation.

Who are the key figures?

Many influential figures are numbered among the renowned deists who followed Herbert. Leading French intellectuals, politicians, and authors such as Voltaire, Napoleon Bonaparte, Victor Hugo, and Jules Verne advocated deism. Adam Smith and Thomas Paine were among the influential intellectual British deists. Many have suggested that John Locke advanced deism more than anyone else in England. However, Locke was technically a rational supernaturalist, neither accepting nor denying all forms of revelation or supernaturalism. In American history, Thomas Jefferson, Benjamin Franklin, and Abraham Lincoln were deists. In the twentieth century, astronaut Neil Armstrong professed belief in deism. Due to a lack of formal proselytizing, classically defined deism has few adherents in our day. However, many have argued that "moralistic therapeutic deism" (MTD) is the main religious belief system in America today. MTD is a form of functional deism.[3]

What are the main beliefs?

Deism has five essential beliefs:

I. **A Supreme Being:** Deism teaches that there is one Supreme God who made all things and who watches over the world. This God has been likened to a great clockmaker who winds the world up like a clock and lets it run by its own laws, not interfering once he has started the process. In deistic thought, reason—apart from revelation—leads one to the Supreme God. Deists deny the deity of Christ, suggesting that the belief that there are three persons in the one true God is irrational. Although deism tends to stress God's nonintervention in the world, some deists have had a view of providence in which God is guiding His creation. Still, they have not held to the full-orbed biblical doctrine of providence.

II. **Worship:** Deism calls mankind to worship the one Supreme God, but deists differ as to what this looks like. Many of them believe that worship consists in the pursuit of a virtuous life. Some deists have held to a view of the Supreme God that led them to pray; others have not.

III. **Morality:** In the deistic worldview, virtue is the highest goal of man. We are acceptable to the Supreme God by right living. All people have the same sense of virtue and know how we ought to live, especially in our relationship with our fellow human beings.

IV. **Repentance:** People appease the Supreme God by

grieving over those things that they know they have done wrong. Deists see no place for a God who requires a blood sacrifice to satisfy His justice.

V. **Immortality:** Deists have differed on whether human beings have an immortal soul and on the existence of the afterlife. Many deists have denied immortality, while others have affirmed it. Deists who affirm the existence of an afterlife have generally held that all humanity may attain to eternal life by doing what is right. In other words, good or virtuous people go to heaven when they die. Deism is essentially a works-righteousness, moralistic religion.

Why do people believe this form of false teaching?

In the age of the Enlightenment, deism was extremely appealing to Western civilization. It offered a rational alternative to historic biblical Christianity. Additionally, deism offered modern people a religion that appeared to be more charitable than Christianity. Moralistic therapeutic deism offers people a God who does not meddle too much in their lives and who also encourages them to be good, fair, and nice to one another. It guarantees salvation to those who pursue a life of goodness and kindness.

How does it hold up against biblical Christianity?

Though God reveals Himself in the things that He has made (Rom. 1:19–20), we can know Him as Savior only through the revelation of Christ in the Scriptures (Luke 16:29, 31; 24:27, 32, 45; Rom. 10:14). The world was created by the word of God's power (Heb. 11:3). He upholds it by that same word (Col. 1:17; Heb. 1:3). God is intimately involved in the governance of every action and event in the world. As Dr. R.C. Sproul said, "If there is one single maverick molecule in this universe running around loose, totally free of God's sovereignty, then we have no guarantee that a single promise of God will ever be fulfilled." Salvation is a free gift of God, not based on anything that we do.

In contrast to the five main beliefs of deism, Scripture teaches the following:

I. **The Supreme Being:** There is only one true and living God, subsisting in three distinct persons: the Father, the Son, and the Holy Spirit. Each member of the Godhead is worthy of our worship, since all the members of the Godhead are "the same in substance, equal in power and glory."[4] The Father is God (1 Cor. 1:3; Gal. 1:3; Eph. 1:2), the Son is God (John 1:1; 8:58; 10:30; Phil. 2:6; Col. 1:15–16; Heb. 1:1–3), and the Spirit is God (Acts 5:3–4). These three persons are distinct, yet they do not constitute three different gods, for they share the one divine essence fully and equally.

II. **Worship:** God alone is worthy of our worship. We are to worship God only according to His revealed truth. John 4:24 says, "God is spirit, and those who worship him must worship in spirit and truth." No one can come into the presence of God without a mediator. As God and man, Jesus is the only mediator between God and man (1 Tim. 2:5). Jesus said: "I am the way, and the truth, and the life. No one comes to the Father except through me" (John 14:6).

III. **Morality:** All people (except Christ) have sinned and fallen short of the glory of God (Rom. 3:23). There is nothing that we in ourselves can do that will bring us into a right relationship with God. God has provided redemption in Christ. Scripture teaches that God justifies us freely—declares us righteous and forgives us—by His grace through the redemption that is in Christ. Salvation is by faith alone through grace alone, apart from works (Eph. 2:8–9). We do not seek to live morally upright lives in order to be accepted by God. We are accepted by God and, therefore, we seek to live lives of grateful obedience, obeying God's moral law (Eph. 2:10).

IV. **Repentance:** Though God commands all people everywhere to repent of their sins (Acts 17:30), our repentance does not atone for sin. God sent Christ to be the perfect and all-sufficient sacrifice for our sins (Heb. 7:27; 9:26). The blood of Jesus covers all our offenses against God (1 John 1:7).

V. **Immortality:** No one goes to heaven because of his works. Rather, whoever believes in the Son of God will have eternal life (John 3:15–16, 36; 6:47). Salvation is a free gift of God's grace in Christ. Jesus lived a perfectly sinless life in order to fulfill the demands of God's law as the representative of God's people (2 Cor. 5:21; Gal. 4:3–4). Jesus died under the wrath of God to take the punishment of His people, and His perfect obedience is credited to those who believe in Him, meaning that believers have eternal life because of the good He has done. God reserves heaven for those who trust in the Son's finished work of redemption (1 Peter 1:3–5).

How can I share the gospel with those who hold to this false teaching?

I. **Focus on God's sovereign power in governing all His creation.** To deny God's providential working in His creation is to deny God Himself. If the sovereign Creator is not working out His plan according to His most wise counsel, chance is ultimate. Scripture teaches that God is not detached from His creation but intervenes in the lives of His creatures. Rather than living in detachment from God, we are called in Scripture to be reconciled to God through the saving work of Jesus. The transcendent God draws near to us in the person of Jesus Christ and by the powerful working of His Spirit.

II. **Focus on the sinfulness of man.** If someone insists that God accepts us because of our goodness, we should remind them of what Scripture says about the sinfulness of man. We are fallen in Adam and are under the wrath and curse of God (Rom. 5:12–21; Gal. 3:13). We are born dead in sins and trespasses (Eph. 2:1–4) and are unable to do anything spiritually acceptable to God in our sinful nature. Any attempt to gain God's approval is a manifestation of self-righteousness. Nothing we do can bring us into a right relationship with God.

III. **Focus on the perfection of Christ's person and saving work.** Only in Christ does God accept sinners. Jesus is God in the flesh, and He took the sin of His people on Himself at the cross in order to reconcile us to God and make us righteous before Him (Rom. 3:21–26; 2 Cor. 5:21; 1 Tim. 3:16; 1 Peter 2:4; 3:18).

Jesus took the infinite wrath of God to atone for all the sin of His people. Because Jesus has borne the punishment that His people deserve, all those who trust in Him alone for salvation will not suffer eternal death but rather will inherit eternal life.

—

MORALISTIC THERAPEUTIC DEISM

Moralistic therapeutic deism is a term coined by sociologists Christian Smith and Melinda Lundquist Denton in their book *Soul Searching: The Religious and Spiritual Lives of American Teenagers* (2005). It refers to a variety of functional deism that, though it is not a complete or formal religious system, is sometimes characterized as the main belief system in America, especially among young people. MTD has five central beliefs: a God exists; He wants people to be good to each other; the goal of life is to be happy; God does not involve Himself in human affairs except to resolve problems; and good people go to heaven when they die.

EDWARD HERBERT

▶ 1583–1648

Edward Herbert, 1st Baron Herbert of Cherbury was an English politician, soldier, diplomat, poet, and philosopher. Educated at Oxford, Herbert served as a member of Parliament, as a soldier in various European campaigns, and as ambassador to France, where he successfully negotiated the marriage of Henrietta Maria to the future King Charles I of England. In his book *De Veritate* (*On Truth*; 1624), Herbert sought to establish reason as the safest guide in finding truth; he rejected revelation as a source of truth and sought instead to construct a natural religion.

LEGALISM AND ANTINOMIANISM

What are legalism and antinomianism?

The terms *legalism* and *antinomianism* describe two false teachings regarding the relationship between the law and the gospel. Legalism is the insistence that a person is accepted by God on the basis of his law keeping. It teaches that we are declared righteous before God through our own observance of either God's law or man-made rules and regulations. Antinomianism says that God does not require a believer to obey the moral law (i.e., the Ten Commandments). In its more extreme and perverted form, antinomianism permits immoral behavior based on the leniency of grace.

When did they begin?

Legalism and antinomianism are rooted in the fall of Adam. All mankind is predisposed to these two moral and theological errors. Accordingly, countless forms of legalism and antinomianism have surfaced throughout history. Legalism and antinomianism undergird all forms of false teaching and heresy.

Who are the key figures?

Legalism

Jesus rebuked the religious leaders in Israel for their hypocritical, self-righteous teaching and lives (Matt. 23:4; Luke 18:9). The Apostle Paul stridently defended the gospel against the doctrinal legalism with which the early church was infected (Gal. 1–3; 1 Tim. 1:6–7).

The Roman Catholic Church has long promoted an elaborate system of religious legalism, which is most evident in its monastic asceticism, penitential system, sacramentalism, and emphasis on merit.[5] Roman Catholicism denies the biblical doctrine of justification by faith alone in Christ alone, teaching that a person is justified by faith in Christ together with his Spirit-wrought good works.

Doctrinal and practical legalism has surfaced in evangelical and Protestant churches over the centuries. By imposing obligations on members to observe man-made rules and regulations, many churches have advanced a form of man-centered legalism (Col. 2:20–23).

In recent decades, proponents of the New Perspective(s) on Paul have taught that a person's final right standing before God is based on his obedience to God's commands.

False religions such as Islam, Judaism, and Buddhism, because they teach a works-based salvation wherein we enter heaven or experience Nirvana because of our good deeds, are non-Christian forms of legalism.

Antinomianism

In the early church, certain false teachers promoted the idea that God's grace tolerates lawless living (see 2 Peter and Jude). Some wickedly dismissed sexual immorality in the name of grace (Jude 4). The Apostle John contended against antinomian ideas in his first letter (1 John 2:4).

"

FOR OUR SAKE
HE MADE HIM TO
BE SIN WHO KNEW
NO SIN, SO THAT
IN HIM WE MIGHT
BECOME THE
RIGHTEOUSNESS
OF GOD.

2 CORINTHIANS 5:21

Throughout church history, antinomianism has appeared in less overt and perverse forms than that in which it appeared in the early church. Martin Luther wrote *Against the Antinomians* to refute the erroneous teaching of the neo-Lutheran antinomian Johannes Agricola. Edward Fisher wrote *The Marrow of Modern Divinity* to address the undercurrents of legalism and antinomianism in certain streams of the Puritan movement. This book was also at the center of a debate over antinomianism in the Church of Scotland in the eighteenth century.[6] In the twentieth century, notable dispensational teachers promoted a form of antinomianism called "easy-believism."

What are the main beliefs?

In the church, legalism surfaces when people teach or believe these ideas:

I. **Get in by grace; stay in by law keeping.** While most forms of legalism in the church deny strict merit in the sense that they affirm the necessity of grace, almost all insist that an individual's good works are necessary for his final justification before God on judgment day. Roman Catholicism teaches that a person is initially justified at baptism;[7] however, his final right standing before God is dependent on a life of continued adherence to religious rituals and Spirit-wrought good works.

II. **Meriting righteousness.** Legalism teaches that people can cooperate with God in order to gain a right standing by their works. Though this view does not involve strict merit, it still reflects a meritorious scheme of salvation. Legalism is often accompanied by a self-righteous spirit in those who advance it. As Luke explained, the Pharisees "trusted in themselves that they were righteous, and treated others with contempt" (Luke 18:9). The Jews of Paul's day were "seeking to establish their own . . . righteousness" (Rom. 10:3).

Antinomianism is evident in these two beliefs:

I. **Grace, not law.** Antinomianism teaches that because God's grace is greater than all our sin, we are no longer under any obligation to obey God's law. If good works do not figure into our justification—our being declared righteous in God's sight—they are unnecessary in the Christian life. Much antinomian teaching denies that someone can displease God by his disobedience. Accordingly, believers no longer need to heed the warnings in Scripture.

II. **Justification only.** Many forms of antinomianism focus solely on justification by faith alone in Christ and thereby functionally deny sanctification. In the teaching of neo-Lutheran antinomianism, faith does not result in a believer's following paths of obedience to God. In dispensational antinomianism, the Ten Commandments have been fulfilled by Christ and are no longer binding on believers.

Why do people believe this form of false teaching?

Our depraved human hearts gravitate toward legalism and lawlessness. The inclination to earn salvation is rooted in our sin nature. Legalism feeds on the sinful pride of mankind by offering a way to make up for the wrongs we have done.

Legalism convinces the consciences of people that they have in themselves what they need to attain righteousness before God and men.

Antinomianism works on people's consciences by convincing them that God does not require us to turn from our wicked ways. Antinomianism presents a Christianity that requires no personal effort or spiritual striving against sin. It offers a counterfeit freedom to the true freedom that Christ gives believers.

How does it hold up against biblical Christianity?

In contrast to the two main doctrines of legalism, Scripture teaches the following:

1.   We do not begin the Christian life by trusting in Christ and then bring it to completion by our works (Gal. 3:1–4; Eph. 1:3–14; Phil. 1:6). Justification is a once-for-all, irreversible act of God by which He forgives all the sins of believers and accepts them as righteous only because of the imputed righteousness of

"

I DO NOT NULLIFY
THE GRACE OF
GOD, FOR IF
RIGHTEOUSNESS
WERE THROUGH
THE LAW, THEN
CHRIST DIED FOR
NO PURPOSE.

GALATIANS 2:21

Christ (Gen. 15:6; Rom. 3:21–22; 4:1–5). The sanctification of a Christian does not add to his standing before God. Believers cannot lose their standing before God because of their sin, though God may chasten them for it.

II. The law of God requires perfect obedience (Gal. 3:10–11). Christ was born subject to the law in order to merit perfect righteousness for His people (Gal. 4:4). As the representative last Adam, Jesus obeyed the law of God perfectly. In the place where Adam sinned, Jesus obeyed. God produces good works in believers after He accepts them in Christ, but these works do not factor into their standing before Him (Eph. 2:8–10).

Contrary to the two main doctrines of antinomianism, Scripture teaches the following:

I. God's justifying grace is greater than all our sin (Rom. 5:21), and it leads to holiness in the lives of those whom He has justified. The Apostle Paul defended the gospel against the charge of antinomianism by explaining that the believer's union with Christ results in holiness (Rom. 6:1–14). Paul often defended the role of the law in the life of a Christian (Rom. 13:9; Eph. 6:1). Although no one is justified by law keeping, believers fulfill God's law through love (Gal. 5:14). Every believer is to take the warnings of God with the utmost seriousness (1 Cor. 6:9–10).

II. In justification, Jesus atones for the guilt of our sins. In sanctification, Jesus, who has broken the power of sin, enables us to live more and more for Him (Rom. 6:6–10). While justification is a once-for-all act of God, sanctification is an ongoing process in the life of a believer. Christians are called to work out in their Christian lives what God is working in them (Phil. 2:12–13). This includes actively pursuing a life of holiness and obedience to God's commandments.

How can I share the gospel with those who hold to these forms of false teaching?

I. **Focus on the many rejections of these errors in Scripture.** Scripture constantly addresses the false teachings of legalism and lawlessness. In the Old Testament, God always calls rebellious Israel to repentance for their lawless deeds. In the Gospels, Jesus continually rebukes the religious leaders of Israel for their legalism. In the Epistles, the Apostles address the dangerous false teachings of both legalism and lawlessness. The more we direct others to Scripture to see the prevalence of these errors, the more we will be able to help convince them of the danger of embracing them and to give them the gospel remedy.

II. **Focus on the biblical teaching about the depravity of the human heart.** Since legalism and antinomianism stem from the sinful depravity of the human heart, we can help others move away from these errors by pointing to what the Scriptures teach about our sinful condition. The Bible teaches that all people by nature are "dead in . . . trespasses and sins" (Eph. 2:1–5). In ourselves, we are unable to do anything spiritually pleasing to God (Rom. 5:6; Eph. 2:12). All our deeds apart from Christ are violations of God's law, for which we deserve God's eternal wrath and judgment (Matt. 7:23).

III. **Focus on the sufficiency of the person and work of Christ.** The message of Christ crucified cures legalism and antinomianism. Jesus died to deal with our self-righteousness and lawlessness. Christ came as the last Adam (Rom. 5:12–21). We have no righteousness apart from Him. When we come to see that we receive His imputed righteousness by faith alone, we will stop seeking to establish a righteousness by our performance (Phil. 3:9). As we recognize that Jesus died to atone for our lawlessness (1 John 3:4), we will desire to live a life of obedience to His commandments. When we understand that Christ is the source of sanctification for believers (1 Cor. 1:30), we long to be conformed more and more to His image.

—

THE MARROW CONTROVERSY

T he Marrow Controversy was a dispute in the Church of Scotland during the eighteenth century that concerned the relationships between law and gospel and between legalism and anti-nomianism. It was sparked by a statement known as the

Auchterarder Creed: "It is not sound and orthodox to teach that we must forsake sin in order to our coming to Christ." In 1717, a ministerial candidate refused to affirm the statement, which exposed a division in the church. The General Assembly condemned the statement, drawing objections from the group called the Marrow Men; they were opposed by the Neonomians, who saw faith and repentance as fulfilling the legal conditions of the "new law" that were necessary for salvation. The Marrow Men's name comes from the book *The Marrow of Modern Divinity*, written by Edward Fisher and republished in 1718. The book charted a course between legalism and antinomianism; it was banned by the General Assembly but was promoted by Thomas Boston, who wrote and published extensive notes on it.

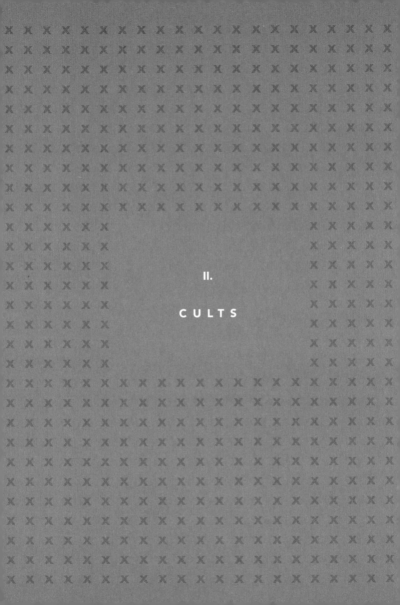

II.

CULTS

INTRODUCTION TO

CULTS

Scholars have frequently used the word *cult* as a common designation for a religious community that has developed around a new set of beliefs and practices. In recent centuries, numerous religious cults and sects have served as competitors to biblical Christianity. In common usage among Christians, the word *cult* usually carries with it the idea of a counterfeit religion with elements of Christian teaching together with new and unbiblical teaching by a compelling founding figure. Cults of this kind are religious organizations that associate themselves with the Bible yet substantially deviate from biblical Christianity as it is outlined in the historic creeds and confessions of the Christian faith. There are three common features to every cult: first, a hierarchical, authoritarian structure of leadership; second, an extremely narrow set of doctrines and practices to which the consciences of the members are bound by the leadership of the movement; and third, an adherence to extrabiblical revelation (generally originating with the founding leader of the movement) or belief that the founding figure of the cult or the organization alone has interpreted the Bible correctly. When we keep these features in mind as we reflect on the various religious movements that are associated with the Bible and that attempt to define themselves as Christian, we will be able to rightly identify cults and defend the faith against their unbiblical doctrines and practices.

In his 1963 work *The Four Major Cults*, Anthony Hoekema drew attention to the teaching and practice of four aberrant religious cults: the Church of Jesus Christ of Latter-day Saints (Mormons), Seventh-day Adventism, Christian Science, and Jehovah's Witnesses. The Mormons, Christian Scientists, Seventh-day Adventists, and Jehovah's Witnesses all have their roots in the nineteenth century and originated in close geographical proximity in the context of the religious enthusiasm of revivalism. Through the mid-twentieth century, Mormonism, Christian Science, and Jehovah's Witnesses were the most widely recognized cults in America, whereas developments in Seventh-day Adventism led many to remove the Seventh-day Adventists from the list of cults and identify them as an idiosyncratic expression of the Christian faith. With the counterculture movement of the late 1960s, a new wave of smaller communal cults appeared in America, including the People's Temple of the Disciples of Christ, founded by Jim Jones; the Children of God, started by David Berg; and the Branch Davidians, led by David Koresh.

As of 2019, there are approximately twenty-five million members of the three major cults worldwide (Mormonism, Christian Science, and Jehovah's Witnesses). Therefore, it is vital that Christians know both the history and basic beliefs of each of these organizations. Many members of these prominent cults are an integral part of American society, academia, politics, and entertainment. A survey of the history, essential beliefs, and important figures of these groups will help Christians engage with members of these unbiblical religious movements. In this section, we offer a brief summary of the history and teachings of Mormonism, Christian Science, and the Jehovah's Witnesses, contrasting their essential beliefs with the teaching of Scripture and offering a few recommendations for how to more effectively share the gospel with those who have been ensnared by these spiritually destructive organizations. It is our sincere desire that this material will help you to be better equipped to defend the Christian faith against the false teaching of these cults and to be used by the Lord to rescue those who have been led astray by them.

MORMONISM

What is Mormonism?

The Church of Jesus Christ of Latter-day Saints, also known as the LDS Church and as the Mormon church, is one of the largest religious cults in the world. As of 2019, the Mormon religion counts more than 16.3 million members.[8] Mormonism teaches that there are many gods, with the Father, the Son, and the Holy Spirit being three separate gods among many others. Furthermore, it is also possible for humans to ascend to godhood. Obedience to moral laws and observance of religious rituals are central to the Mormon faith.

When did it begin?

The Mormon church was founded by Joseph Smith Jr. Born in Vermont in 1805, Smith attended Methodist and Presbyterian churches growing up. In 1820, Smith claimed to have a revelatory vision of two divine beings who he said were God the Father and Jesus Christ. They taught him that all Protestant denominations were wrong.[9] In 1823, he said that an angel named Moroni showed him several golden plates with religious inscriptions on them. This angel supposedly also gave him a pair of seer stones set in a frame like a pair of spectacles, which he called the Urim and Thummim, with which he could interpret the inscriptions. In 1827, Smith began translating these plates, receiving assistance from his acquaintance Oliver Cowdery. Smith did not translate in a conventional sense by working from the text, but he would instead put his face in a hat and peer through the seer stones, and the English translation would appear before his eyes. Cowdery wrote down what Smith dictated, and the result of this collaborative process was the Book of Mormon.

In 1830, Smith founded an institution that he called

the Church of Christ. In 1838, he changed the name to the Church of Jesus Christ of Latter-day Saints. In addition to the Book of Mormon, Smith wrote most of another book of Mormon scriptures called the Doctrine and Covenants and a final book of scriptures called the Pearl of Great Price. Smith moved around the country until officials arrested him in Illinois in 1844 for treason, public disruption, and polygamy. A lynch mob stormed the prison and killed Smith and his brother Hyrum. Brigham Young, a leader in the early Mormon community, succeeded Smith after a succession crisis and led Smith's disciples to the Great Salt Lake basin in the Utah territory, where they founded Salt Lake City.

Who are the key figures?

Seventeen presidents have presided over the Church of Jesus Christ of Latter-day Saints since its inception. Next to Smith, Young—the second president of the church—is the most prominent figure in the church's history.

There have been numerous influential Mormons in education, media, entertainment, sports, and politics. Among the most celebrated Mormon athletes are NFL quarterback Steve Young (a descendant of Brigham Young); heavyweight boxing champion Jack Dempsey; and NBA player, coach, and executive Danny Ainge. Former U.S. senators Harry Reid and Orrin Hatch are practicing Mormons. Senator Mitt Romney is one of the most recognized members of the LDS Church today. Prominent current and former Mormons in entertainment include Glenn Beck, Aaron Eckhart, Gladys Knight, and Donny and Marie Osmond.

What are the main beliefs?

Mormonism has four main beliefs:

I. **Continuing revelation.** The four written sources of revelation in the LDS Church are the Book of Mormon, the Doctrine and Covenants, the Pearl of Great Price, and the King James Version of the Bible. However, in Mormonism, divine revelation is not limited to these books but also includes the utterances of living prophets. The church has developed its doctrine and practice over time, even after the death of its founder.

"

AS MAN NOW IS,

GOD ONCE WAS;

AS GOD NOW IS,

MAN MAY BE.

LORENZO SNOW

Its president is considered a living prophet, and individual members are encouraged to seek personal revelation. According to the church, "Latter-day Saints believe in an open scriptural canon, which means that there are other books of scripture besides the Bible (such as the Book of Mormon) and that God continues to reveal His word through living prophets."[10]

II. **Humanized deity.** Belief in a plurality of gods, who preexisted as material spirits, is foundational to LDS belief. The God of this world was once a man who became a god. Smith said: "God himself was once as we are now and is an exalted man. . . . We have imagined and supposed that God was God from all eternity. I will refute that idea. . . . God himself, the Father of us all, dwelt on an earth, the same as Jesus Christ himself did."[11] As God ascended to godhood, so also righteous men and women can become gods. This idea was summarized by former church president Lorenzo Snow like this: "As man now is, God once was; as God now is, man may be."[12]

Jesus is the eternally begotten Son of God; however, He is not the supreme God. Smith wrote, "The Apostles have discovered that there were Gods above . . . there being a God above, the Father of our Lord Jesus Christ."[13] According to Smith, Jesus was an eternal spirit being, who—together with his spirit brother Lucifer—was made incarnate to be tested and to become a god.

III. **Preexistent humanity.** Every human existed before birth as an eternal spirit child. Smith taught, "Man, as a spirit, was begotten and born of heavenly parents, and reared to maturity in the eternal mansions of the Father, prior to coming upon the earth in a temporal body."[14] Man should seek to become a god in the afterlife by living a righteous life.

IV. **Atonement and afterlife.** Mormons believe that Jesus is the Redeemer who died on the cross not to atone for sin but to guarantee the resurrection of all people. After death, people's souls go to the spirit world, where they await the resurrection and final judgment.

There are three levels of glory to which people may be assigned after the final judgment depending on their acceptance of and obedience to Mormon teachings and ordinances: the telestial kingdom, the terrestrial kingdom, and the celestial kingdom. The outer darkness is reserved for those who do not attain to one of those levels of glory.

Those who reject the Mormon gospel and continue in sin are sent to the telestial kingdom, the lowest of the levels of glory. The spirit inhabitants of the telestial kingdom serve God but cannot come into His presence. When Christ establishes His thousand-year reign on earth, the members of the telestial kingdom will live as imprisoned spirits until the end of that period. Next is the terrestrial kingdom, the destination of those who live good lives but who do not accept the Mormon gospel. Those who enter the terrestrial kingdom experience the presence of Jesus, but not the fullness of God the Father. Only the righteous—those who have lived according to Mormon teachings and have undergone Mormon ordinances—go to the celestial kingdom, where they can become gods who populate their own planets with their spouses. It is possible to move up in levels of glory even after death if one believes the Mormon gospel in the spirit world and vicariously receives Mormon ordinances. Apart from these levels of glory, there is a place called the outer darkness; it is the destination of Satan and his angels, along with humans who have committed the unpardonable sin (often thought to be apostasy from Mormonism).

Why do people believe this form of false teaching?

Smith's followers considered him a martyr. In the eighteenth century, persecution of sects and cults in America gave traction to the end-time hope of Mormon disciples. Today, Mormonism's growth is due to the church's proselytization. All Mormon men are trained and sent on a two-year mission. Mormonism promotes large families and presents a portrait of wholesome family values often lacking in our society. The moralism of the Mormon religion is one of its most appealing features to the unregenerate.

How does it hold up against biblical Christianity?

In contrast to the four main beliefs of Mormonism, Scripture teaches the following:

I. The Old and New Testaments alone are the inspired and infallible revelation of God written (2 Tim. 3:16; 2 Peter 1:20–21). God has given grave warnings about adding to or subtracting from His Word (Rev. 22:18–19). The Bible teaches that many false prophets will propagate destructive heresies (Matt. 7:15; 24:11, 24; 2 Peter 2:1; 1 John 4:1). The Apostle Paul charged believers to be diligent in preserving the truth of the gospel against false gospels proclaimed by men or angels (Gal. 1:8).

II. The God of Scripture is the true and living God (Deut. 6:4; 29:18; Ps. 96:5; 1 Thess. 1:9). God was, is, and forever will be the eternally unchangeable God (Ex. 3:14; Mal. 3:6; John 8:58). God is spirit and eternally exists in three persons (Matt. 28:19; John 4:24; 2 Cor. 13:14). Jesus is the second person of the

Godhead and is God incarnate (John 1:14). The Son is equal to the Father and the Spirit in all things (John 1:1; 10:30; Rom. 9:5; Phil. 2:6; Heb. 1:3).

III. God made us in His own image, in knowledge, righteousness, and holiness (Gen. 1:26; Eph. 4:24; Col. 3:10). Man did not exist before creation. Scripture nowhere teaches that people become gods.

IV. Jesus died in the place of His people on the cross in order to atone for their sins (1 Cor. 15:3; 2 Cor. 5:21; 1 Peter 2:24) and propitiate the wrath of God (Rom. 5:9; 8:1; 1 Thess. 1:10; 1 John 2:2). Jesus died to save His people from their sins and from eternal wrath (Matt. 1:21). On the last day, all who believe in Christ will be raised to eternal life (Mark 10:30; John 3:15–16, 36; 5:24), and all who did not believe will be raised to everlasting punishment in hell (Matt. 18:8; 25:46; Mark 9:44; 2 Thess. 1:9; Jude 6–7).

How can I share the gospel with those who hold to this false teaching?

I. **Focus on the infallibility, inerrancy, and authority of Scripture.** The Scriptures of the Old and New Testament are the only infallible, inerrant, and authoritative Word of God (Prov. 30:5; John 17:17; 2 Tim. 3:16; 2 Peter 1:20–21). If possible, work from the King James Version of Scripture when witnessing to Mormons. Because Mormons use the KJV, using it in encounters with Mormons will make witnessing to them much easier than trying to do so with a modern English version. Focus on the Bible's closing prohibition against continuing revelation (Rev. 22:18–19).

II. **Focus on the scriptural truth about the triune God.** The Bible's teaching about the Godhead is essential to helping a Mormon see the truth (Matt. 28:19; 2 Cor. 13:14). Explain that the Bible sometimes speaks of the triune God as He is in Himself and sometimes of the various roles of the members of the Godhead in the work of redemption. Explain those passages that speak of the deity of Christ (John 1:1–3; Rom. 9:5; Col. 1:15–16; Heb. 1:1–3, 8–12), as well as those passages that speak of His submissive role as the Mediator in the work of redemption (John 10:29; 1 Cor. 11:3; 1 Tim. 2:5–6).

III. **Focus on the Bible's teaching about the gospel.** Salvation is by grace alone through faith alone in Christ alone (Gal. 1:8; Eph. 2:8–9). Jesus is God "manifested in the flesh" (1 Tim. 3:16; see John 1:14). A mere created being could never substitute himself for the sins of another, let alone for the sins of a multitude. Only Jesus, the infinite and eternal God incarnate, could come and place Himself on the cross as a substitute for the sins of His people. He did not merely make salvation possible by guaranteeing our resurrection; He actually accomplished it for His people through His once-for-all, perfect sacrifice. Salvation is not based on our obedience; it is based entirely on the finished work of Christ.

———

THE BOOK OF MORMON

T he Book of Mormon is one of the four sacred texts of the Church of Jesus Christ of Latter-day Saints. It was first published in 1830 by Joseph Smith. It is purported to be an account of the ancient inhabitants of North America: the Jaredites, the Nephites, and the Lamanites. These groups are said to have originated in the ancient Near East; the Jaredites made their way to the Americas after the Tower of Babel event, while the Nephites and Lamanites made their journey shortly before the fall of Jerusalem in 586 BC. The climax of the book is the appearance of the risen Christ in the book of III Nephi, which Mormons see as fulfilling His words about "other sheep that are not of this fold" (John 10:16). Jesus' appearance ushered in a renaissance, but the inhabitants soon devolved into warring factions again. The book is said to have been compiled by a man named Moroni, who hid the records in what is now New York state. He appeared as an angel to Smith and guided him to the plates and gave him the means to translate them from "reformed Egyptian."

CHRISTIAN SCIENCE

What is Christian Science?

Christian Science is a religious movement founded in the nineteenth century and based on the writing of Mary Baker Eddy. She founded the Church of Christ, Scientist, and her book *Science and Health with Key to the Scriptures* serves as the main source of teaching for Christian Science. *Science and Health* contains Eddy's interpretation of portions of Scripture, combined with her teaching on science and mind over matter for physical healing. Today, there are an estimated two thousand Christian Science congregations—often represented by storefront reading rooms on downtown streets—worldwide.

When did it begin?

Mary Ann Morse Baker was born in New Hampshire in 1821. Routinely sick throughout much of her early life, Mary visited mentalist Phineas Quimby in 1864 for instruction in principles of divine mind over matter for physical healing. On February 1, 1866, Mary was seriously injured when she slipped and hit her head on ice. After a doctor told her she had only a few days to live, Mary took a Bible, read about the healing of the paralytic in Matthew 9:1–8, and applied the metaphysical principles of mind over matter she had learned from Quimby. Upon doing so, Mary claimed, she experienced complete healing. This was the beginning of Mary's new religion, which she called Christian Science, insisting that it was merely a retrieval of primitive Christianity. In 1875, Mary founded the Christian Science Publishing Society in order to publish and circulate copies of *Science and Health*. In 1879, she founded the Church of Christ, Scientist.

Who are the key figures?

Though Eddy is the only prominent teacher in the Christian Science church, the church counts among its adherents several well-known figures and people who are connected to well-known figures. Audrey Hepburn, Elizabeth Taylor, Henry Fonda, Robin Williams, Robert Duvall, Kelsey Grammer, Ellen DeGeneres, and the parents of Marilyn Monroe have at some point all been practicing members. Ginger Rogers and Joan Crawford were members of the church until their deaths. Olympic gold medalist gymnast Shannon Miller was brought up in a Christian Science home.

What are the main beliefs?

Due to the highly mystical and philosophical nature of Eddy's writings, it can be challenging to systematize her doctrine. However, the following are central teachings in her writing:

1. **Mystical, anti-trinitarian monotheism.** According to Mary Baker Eddy, mind and intelligence are God.

99

"Intelligence is omniscience, omnipresence, and omnipotence. It is the primal and eternal quality of infinite Mind, of the triune Principle,—Life, Truth, and Love,—named God. . . . Mind is God."[15] Eddy rejected historic Christian Trinitarianism. She wrote, "The theory of three persons in one God (that is, a personal Trinity or Tri-unity) suggests polytheism, rather than the one ever-present I AM."[16] Eddy reduced God to a philosophical universal principle in which all men participate by way of the mind and intellect.[17]

II. **A denial of the fall, sin, misery, and death.** Eddy denied the fall. If God is perfect, man—the idea or reflection of God—is also reflectively perfect. She explained: "God is the creator of man, and, the divine Principle of man remaining perfect, the divine idea or reflection, indestructible, remains perfect. Man is the expression of God's being."[18] Elsewhere she wrote, "Man is in a degree as perfect as the Mind that forms him."[19] Reflecting on sin and misery, Eddy suggested: "To put down the claim of sin, you must detect it, remove the mask, point out the illusion, and thus get

"

THE SICK
ARE NOT HEALED
MERELY BY
DECLARING THERE
IS NO SICKNESS,
BUT BY KNOWING
THAT THERE
IS NONE.

MARY BAKER EDDY

the victory over sin and so prove its unreality. The sick are not healed merely by declaring there is no sickness, but by knowing that there is none."[20] Regarding death, Eddy wrote, "If man believes in death now, he must disbelieve in it when learning that there is no reality in death, since the truth of being is deathless." Eddy taught that if we believe there is such a thing as sin, sickness, and death, then we will be subject to the illusion of such things. If we acknowledge that such things do not exist, then we will be set free from both the illusion and the reality.

III. **A denial of the deity, death, and atonement of Jesus.** Eddy denied the deity of Jesus. She explicitly taught that "Jesus Christ is not God, as Jesus himself declared."[21] Eddy rejected the efficacy of the blood of Jesus. She wrote, "The material blood of Jesus was no more efficacious to cleanse from sin when it was shed upon 'the accursed tree,' than when it was flowing in his veins as he went daily about his Father's business."[22] Eddy taught that Jesus did not truly die. Rather, Jesus

CHRISTIAN SCIENCE

only appeared to die, and by escaping death, He exhibited the supreme act of mind over matter—an act His disciples were to emulate. His example saves humanity from the illusion of sin, sickness, and death.[23] Jesus saves people by exemplifying oneness with God in truth, life, and love.[24]

Why do people believe this form of false teaching?

In an age of religious rationalism and medical progress, Eddy's teaching appealed to those who were looking for spiritual renewal and power over sickness. Uniting her interpretation of Scripture to her teaching on science and metaphysical mentalism, Eddy formulated a religion that would seek a middle ground between "stern Protestantism" and "doubtful liberalism."[25] Her teaching presented a spirituality attainable by the natural mind that avoids the supernaturalism of Protestantism and the antisupernaturalism of liberalism.

How does it hold up against biblical Christianity?

I. **The triune God.** Scripture reveals that there is only one true and living God: "Hear, O Israel: The LORD our God, the LORD is one" (Deut. 6:4). The Bible also clearly teaches that the Father, Son, and Holy Spirit are three distinct persons who subsist within the one God (Matt. 28:19; 1 Cor. 12:4–6; 2 Cor. 13:14; Rev. 1:4–5). These three persons are not three gods. Rather, the three members of the Godhead eternally coexist as the one true and living God.

II. **Sin, misery, and death.** Scripture teaches that sin, misery, and death are the inescapable consequences of Adam's sin. They form the sad experience of life in this fallen world. The Apostle Paul explained, "Just as sin came into the world through one man, and death through sin, and so death spread to all men because all sinned" (Rom. 5:12). In short, "the wages of sin is death" (Rom. 6:23). All the miseries of this life are a result of Adam's first transgression—even death and eternal punishment. To deny the reality of sin is to deceive ourselves. As Scripture says, "If we say we have no sin, we deceive ourselves, and the truth is not in us" (1 John 1:8).

III. **The deity, death, and atonement of Jesus.** The Bible reveals that Jesus is "God over all, blessed forever" (Rom. 9:5). "All the fullness of God was pleased to dwell" in Jesus (Col. 1:19). He is "the radiance of the glory of God and the exact imprint of his nature" (Heb. 1:3). The Son of God incarnate really and truly died on the cross (Phil. 2:8; Heb. 2:9, 14). According to Scripture, the blood of Jesus is efficacious to atone for the sin of all His people (Rom. 5:9; Heb. 9:12; Rev. 1:5). The Bible teaches that "without the shedding of blood there is no forgiveness of sins" (Heb. 9:22).

How can I share the gospel with those who hold to this false teaching?

Although Christian Science is a rapidly declining religion, its view of the unreality of disease and death has some affinities with the prosperity gospel and Word of Faith movements. If one encounters a Christian Scientist, here are two things to focus on when sharing the gospel with him or her:

I. **Focus on the Bible's teaching about sin, misery, and death.** By his disobedience, Adam brought sin, misery, and death into the world (Gen. 3; Rom. 5:12–21). Those who deny the fall of man must be confronted with the inescapable reality of sin and misery in this fallen world. Additionally, highlight what Scripture teaches about sin as a violation of God's law (1 John 3:4). Appeal to Romans 6:23. Consider asking the following questions: If God is All in All, as Eddy suggested, from where does evil originate? If sin and sickness do not exist, why believe that healing can be achieved by prayer unto mind over matter?

II. **Focus on what Scripture reveals about the death of Jesus.** The Scriptures teach that final victory over sin and death comes only through the death of Jesus on the cross. The eternal Son of God became incarnate in order to die for those who would believe in Him. By shedding His blood on the cross, Jesus atoned for the sins of His people (Acts 20:28; Rom. 3:25; 5:9; Heb. 9:12–14; 1 John 1:7). Jesus died in the place of His people under the wrath of God to deliver them from the power of sin and the powers of darkness (Rom. 5:10; 6:10; Heb. 2:9, 14–15), and His victory will be fully manifest when the presence of sin, sickness, and death are removed from the new heaven and earth (Rev. 21). Consider asking the following question: If Jesus claimed to have died in Scripture, as Eddy acknowledged, why does she deny that He truly died?

PHINEAS P. QUIMBY

▶ 1802–66

Phineas P. Quimby was an American mentalist and mesmerist, widely considered the founder of the New Thought movement. New Thought teaches that one's mental state can manifest itself in reality, a belief that often emphasizes that disease is an illusion and that people have the power to heal themselves through positive thinking. Quimby claimed to have healed his tuberculosis through the power of mind over matter. Mary Baker Eddy, founder of Christian Science, was a student of Quimby, but she later claimed that he played no role in her formulating her system. Notably, Eddy's system contains a theistic element that is lacking in Quimby's teaching.

JEHOVAH'S WITNESSES

Who are the Jehovah's Witnesses?

Over the past century and a half, the Jehovah's Witnesses have become one of the most significant cults in the world. As of 2019, an estimated 8.7 million people adhere to the teaching and practice of this false religion worldwide.[26]

When did it begin?

In the late 1870s, Charles Taze Russell—a Restoration movement minister—began publishing his heretical doctrine in a periodical titled *Zion's Watch Tower and Herald of Christ's Presence*. Russell grew up in a religious home, attending both Presbyterian and Congregational churches. As a teenager, however, he started questioning several essential Christian doctrines, such as the Trinity and eternal punishment. Having been a follower of the Adventist movement, an umbrella term for those influenced by nineteenth-century American preacher William Miller and his false prediction of Christ's return in 1843, Russell insisted that Christ returned in nonvisible form in 1874. When his prediction that Christians would be resurrected in 1878 failed, Russell distanced himself from the Adventist movement. Russell started his own publishing company in 1881 called the Watch Tower Bible and Tract Society, which published as many as sixteen million copies of his books and pamphlets by the time of his death in 1916.

Who are the key figures?

In 1916, J.F. Rutherford was elected the second president of the organization. Though considerably less prolific as a writer than Russell, Rutherford took on the role as the unofficial infallible prophet for the organization. When Rutherford died in 1942, N.H. Knorr became the president of the Jehovah's Witnesses. Among the most famous Jehovah's Witness of our day are the late musician Prince and tennis stars Serena and Venus Williams. Michael Jackson and Dwight D. Eisenhower also grew up as Jehovah's Witnesses.

What are the main beliefs?

Jehovah's Witnesses are most well known for denying the Trinity, the deity of Christ, the personhood of the Holy Spirit, and the doctrine of eternal punishment. Their false teaching on these subjects can be summarized under two main headings:

I.   **The Father alone is God.** The Jehovah's Witnesses hold to the sole deity of the Father on the basis that Jehovah (a frequently used English rendering of God's covenant name in Hebrew) is represented as the only God in Scripture. Denying classical Trinitarian doctrine, the Jehovah's Witnesses adamantly reject the idea that there are three persons in the Godhead. In their attack on historic Christian doctrine, the Jehovah's

Witnesses insist that a belief in three persons in the Godhead is equivalent to a belief in three gods.

Since the Jehovah's Witnesses do not believe in the triune God, they teach that Jesus is a created being—specifically, He is the archangel Michael. Although they refer to Him as "the only begotten of God," Jehovah's Witnesses insist that Jesus is the first of the created beings of God. They teach that Jesus agreed to be placed in the womb of the Virgin Mary in order to be a sacrifice for the sins of humanity. However, Jehovah's Witnesses do not believe that Jesus' death propitiated the eternal wrath of God, since they do not believe in the deity of Jesus or in eternal punishment.

According to the Jehovah's Witnesses, the Holy Spirit is not a person, let alone God. Rather, the Spirit is merely an emanating and active force of God.

II. **No eternal punishment.** Jehovah's Witnesses insist that there is no eternal torment for unbelievers in the afterlife. In Jehovah's Witness theology, the body and the soul are inseparable, so the soul dies with the body. Jehovah's Witnesses believe that physical death was the only thing Adam suffered when he fell in the garden. According to the Jehovah's Witnesses, there is no immortal soul.

The Jehovah's Witnesses teach that the 144,000 mentioned in Revelation 7:4 are 144,000 faithful Jehovah's Witnesses who will go to heaven. The remainder of faithful Jehovah's Witnesses will be resurrected and live forever on earth. Those who die without hearing of Christ or knowing God's will in the Bible will be raised in the resurrection of the unrighteous and will have a second chance to believe in the teachings of the Jehovah's Witnesses and obey God and to be included in the final inheritance of eternal life on earth. Anyone who does not attain to the eternal inheritance by failing to believe and obey the teachings of the Jehovah's Witnesses will be annihilated.

Why do people believe this form of false teaching?

The Jehovah's Witnesses insist that Scripture is the only source of divine revelation. This leads to the faulty conclusion that the Jehovah's Witnesses are simply teaching the Bible. However, the organization also publishes and distributes millions of copies of *The Watchtower* magazine, which they treat as the infallible interpreter of Scripture, as well as other publications. Proselytizing is the central feature of their religion; the organization equips and sends all its members out into the world to make converts. The Jehovah's Witnesses offer people a moralistic, monotheistic religion. Presenting a picture of morally clean families, good health, and upright behavior, the Jehovah's Witnesses hold to false teaching that can feed a self-righteous spirit. Additionally, the Jehovah's Witnesses are a multiethnic organization, a characteristic that is often lacking in other religious groups.

How does it hold up against biblical Christianity?

I. **The triune God is the true and living God.** Scripture consistently teaches that there are three persons in the Godhead (Matt. 28:19; 2 Cor. 13:14). The Father is God (Isa. 63:16; Luke 11:2; John 4:23). The Son is

God (John 1:1; Rom. 9:5; Col. 1:15–16; Heb. 1:3). The Holy Spirit is also God (Acts 5:3–4). The three persons of the Godhead are not three gods but three persons subsisting in the one God.

The Son of God is fully God. Jesus reveals Himself to be Jehovah (Ex. 3:14; John 8:58). Jesus claimed equality with the Father in the Godhead (John 8:58; 10:30). The Bible teaches that Jesus is God in every way that God is defined as God (Rom. 9:5; Phil. 2:5–6). Scripture reveals that "all things" were made through the Son (John 1:3; Col. 1:16). It is impossible for "all things" to be created by Him if He Himself was created. Scripture teaches that the Holy Spirit is a communicative divine person, the personal agent of supernatural revelation. David said, "The Spirit of the LORD speaks by me" (2 Sam. 23:2). Jesus affirmed the Spirit's personal inspiration of Scripture when He cited Psalm 110, saying, "David, in the Spirit, calls him Lord" (Matt. 22:43). The writer of Hebrews appealed to the Spirit's divine authorship of Psalm 95 when he wrote, "As the Holy Spirit says, 'Today, if you hear his voice'" (Heb. 3:7).

The Apostle Peter acknowledged the deity of the Spirit when he confronted Ananias, saying: "Why has Satan filled your heart to lie to the Holy Spirit? . . . You have not lied to man but to God" (Acts 5:3–4).

The Nicene Creed (the early Christian statement of faith from AD 325) declares what Scripture teaches about the deity of Christ in relationship to the Trinity over against all early church heresies on the Trinity.

II. **Eternal death is the destination of the wicked.**
Scripture teaches that God created man in His image with an immortal soul (Gen. 1:26; Eccl. 12:5–7). God's judgment against man's sin in the garden was eternal death. By his disobedience, Adam brought spiritual, physical, and eternal death on himself and his natural-born descendants (Rom. 5:12–21). Scripture uses the adjective "eternal" to qualify the nature of the punishment due to man for his sin (Jer. 20:11; Matt. 18:8; 25:46; 2 Thess. 1:9; Jude 6–7; see also Dan. 12:2; Mark 9:44). The idea that God annihilates the souls of men is contrary to the biblical teaching on the eternal justice of God. God the Son became incarnate to propitiate

(satisfy) the eternal wrath of God for His people by His death on the cross. Jesus came to give eternal life to all those who trust Him for salvation (John 3:15–18). All sinners deserve eternal death—everlasting punishment—but Jesus rescues from this end everyone who trusts in Him alone.

How can I share the gospel with those who hold to this false teaching?

I. **Focus on what the Bible teaches about the deity of Christ.** The Jehovah's Witnesses have their own highly inaccurate translation of Scripture—the New World Translation—that empties God's Word of its many references to the deity of Christ. However, there are still several passages in it that are translated properly that attribute deity to the Son. You can take a Jehovah's Witness to Isaiah 9:6 in the New World Translation and point out that the name of the promised Messiah is "Mighty God." The New World Translation has also sought to change the wording of Hebrews 1, since it clearly attributes deity to Christ. However, in Hebrews 1:8, God the Father addresses the Son by the name Jehovah, citing Psalm 102:25–26. This is biblical evidence that Jesus is Jehovah. Finally, although the Jehovah's Witnesses have attempted to strip from the Bible its many clear references to Jesus' receiving worship from His disciples, Luke 24:52 is one passage they cannot avoid. Only God is to be worshiped. Jesus received worship; therefore, Jesus is God. However, while every English translation of Scripture rightly reads "they worshiped him" in Luke 24:52, the New World Translation reads "they did obeisance to him."

II. **Focus on the scriptural teaching about the just punishment for sin.** Scripture teaches that "the wages of sin is death" (Rom. 6:23). Physical death leads to eternal death for those under the wrath and curse of God. Jesus and the Apostles taught that the just penalty for sin is "eternal punishment" (Matt. 25:46; see also 2 Thess. 1:9; Jude 7). God is infinite and eternal; therefore, one sin against the infinite and eternal God deserves infinite and eternal punishment. Coming to terms with what our sin deserves is essential to seeing our need for the atoning sacrifice of the God-man, Jesus Christ. Conversely, if there is no eternal punishment, men should simply desire to live their lives for possessions and pleasure (1 Cor. 15:32).

Nineteen fourteen is an important year in the eschatology of Jehovah's Witnesses. Being born of the Millerite tradition, the Witnesses focused on date setting as an important aspect of their theology from the beginning, and several prophecies regarding eschatological events came and went without incident during the first few decades of the group's history. Witness publications initially predicted that Christ would return to destroy nominal Christianity and usher in Armageddon in October 1914. When that failed to materialize, the prediction was amended to state that He had instead returned invisibly and set up His reign in heaven, marking the beginning of a time of judgment on mankind.

—

NEW WORLD TRANSLATION

The New World Translation is a translation of the Bible produced by the Jehovah's Witnesses, first published in 1950 (New Testament) and 1961 (whole Bible) and extensively revised in 2013. Though it is not the first Jehovah's Witness translation, it was the first to be translated from the original biblical languages. In turn, it has itself been translated into 184 languages worldwide, including twenty-nine from the 2013 revision. It is notable for its idiosyncratic translation choices that are often seen as serving Witness theology—particularly, "the Word was a god" in John 1:1—and for its use of the name *Jehovah* for the divine name *Yahweh*. *Jehovah* is even used in the New Testament, where the divine name does not appear; instead, *Jehovah* translates *kyrios* (lord).

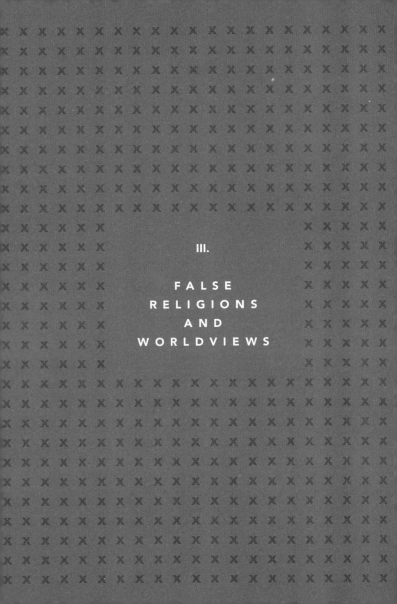

III.

FALSE
RELIGIONS
AND
WORLDVIEWS

FALSE RELIGIONS
AND WORLDVIEWS

Old covenant Israel dwelled in close proximity to nations that worshiped and served false gods. Accordingly, God continually warned His people throughout the old covenant period about the danger of succumbing to the influence of false religions and their practices (Ex. 34:15; Deut. 6:14; 7:3–4, 16; 11:16, 28; 13:6–8; 20:18; Josh. 24:20; 1 Sam. 7:3; 1 Kings 9:1–9; 2 Kings 17:7–23; 2 Chron. 36:1–21; Jer. 16:1–13). Instead of heeding these warnings, however, Israel's kings and people repeatedly gave themselves over to the false religions and worship of neighboring nations. In one sense, the Old Testament is a record of the long, sad history of Israel's idolatry. The Old Testament explains the worthlessness of idols and false religions (1 Kings 18:20–40; Isa. 44:9; Jer. 10). Yet, it also reveals that they are the products of demonic influence (Lev. 17:7; Deut. 32:12; 2 Chron. 11:15; Ps. 106:37). Scripture teaches us that false religions exist because Satan is "a liar and the father of lies" (John 8:44). Indeed, Satan often "disguises himself as an angel of light" (2 Cor. 11:14), inspiring false religions that may have in some ways an outward form of godliness but actually deny its power (2 Tim. 3:1–9).

In the new covenant, Jesus gave His disciples a commission to carry the gospel to the nations (Matt. 28:19). As the Apostles went to preach the gospel among the nations, they encountered a diversity of false religions in many of the cities and regions where they ministered (Acts 14:8–18; 17:16–34; 19:23–41). Luke tells us that the Apostle Paul's spirit was provoked within him when he saw the multiplicity of idols and false religions in the city of Athens (17:16). In response to this evident idolatry, Paul addressed the spiritual ignorance of the people (vv. 22–23). He then preached the truth of God and of the resurrection of Christ to them (vv. 22–34).

The New Testament reveals how God is redeeming a people from their idolatry and false religions (1 Thess. 1:9–10).

False religions are as widespread today as they were in the days of old covenant Israel and throughout the Apostolic age. Presently, nearly 85 percent of the world's population claim devotion to one of 4,200 religions worldwide.[27] Among those who profess religious allegiance, most adhere to one of the twelve major world religions—Christianity, Judaism, Islam, Hinduism, Buddhism, Sikhism, Confucianism, Taoism, the Baha'i faith, Shinto, Jainism, and Zoroastrianism. A growing number of those who do not hold to a particular religion profess to be atheists, agnostics, skeptics, or secularists. Though these do not technically constitute a "religious group," researchers have determined this group to be the second-largest religious group in North America and in many parts of Europe.[28] In recent years, many of these religiously unaffiliated have been classified as "nones," since they do not profess devotion to any particular religion.

Placed side by side with Christianity, false religions and worldviews often have deceptively similar ethics and practices. In his letter to the Colossians, the Apostle Paul reflected on the deceptive nature of false teaching. He warned believers about counterfeit religions that have "an appearance of wisdom in promoting self-made religion and asceticism and severity to the body" (Col. 2:23). However, all false religions are anti-Christian at their core. The Apostle John explained: "Who is the liar but he who denies that Jesus is the Christ? This is the antichrist, he who denies the Father and the Son. No one who denies the Son has the Father" (1 John 2:22–23).

In order to more effectively defend the Christian faith against the attacks of false religions and anti-Christian worldviews, Christians should know something of the origins and essential beliefs of the major false religions. Additionally, we should be able to discern how the beliefs of false religions differ from the essential Christian doctrines that have been revealed by the triune God in Scripture. In this section, we will consider the history and essential beliefs of three of the world's major false religions (Buddhism, Hinduism, and Islam) and two prevalent anti-Christian worldviews (New Age spirituality, and atheism and secularism). We will then compare their essential beliefs with the teaching of Scripture. Finally, we will offer a few suggestions for sharing the gospel with those who have embraced these false religions and anti-Christian world-views. It is our sincere desire that this will serve as a helpful guide as you seek to live as a faithful witness to God's grace in Christ in the gospel.

BUDDHISM

What is Buddhism?

The fourth-largest religion in the world, Buddhism is an ancient religion with its origins on the Indian subcontinent. There are several branches and sub-branches of Buddhism (including Theravada, Mahasamghika, Vajrayana, Nichiren, Shingon, and Zen), but they are all *monistic* rather than monotheistic. That is, Buddhism is built on the belief in the absolute unity of all things and the balancing of opposites in the one reality. In Buddhism, all reality is ultimately one, and there is no such thing as the Creator-creature distinction (see below). An estimated five hundred million people practice Buddhism today.

When did it begin?

There is considerable disagreement over the details of Buddhism's origins. However, scholars agree that it was founded in the fourth or fifth century BC by Siddhartha Gautama, who came to be known as the Buddha. Gautama, a young prince from northern India, noted the contrast between the materialism of his upbringing and the suffering, sickness, and death he observed around him. Consequently, he began questioning the meaning of suffering. In the hope of understanding these things, Gautama left his home, wife, and son to find mentors to teach him the principles of the ascetic life and meditation. Gautama achieved enlightenment after meditating for forty days and forty nights under a fig tree (now known as the Bodhi Tree, or "tree of awakening"). He claimed to have seen the planet Venus on the horizon and realized that he was looking at himself (since all is one). He spent the next forty-five years traveling through northern India, spreading the principles he gained from his experience of enlightenment. After Gautama's death, a powerful Indian emperor named King Ashoka (274–232 BC) converted to Buddhism and ensured its establishment throughout ancient Asia.

Who are the key figures?

Over the millennia, myriad famous Buddhist teachers, scholars, and monks have promoted various forms of Buddhist teaching. The most well-known Buddhist today is the fourteenth Dalai Lama, Tenzin Gyatso, whose title is used for the spiritual leader of a particular branch of Tibetan Buddhism.

Several famous businessmen, athletes, musicians, authors, activists, movie producers, actors, and actresses have been practicing Buddhists, including Richard Gere, Steve Jobs, Tiger Woods, Leonard Cohen, David Bowie, Jack Kerouac, Rosa Parks, George Lucas, Oliver Stone, Goldie Hawn, Jeff Bridges, Brad Pitt, Jennifer Aniston, and Kate Hudson.

What are the main beliefs?

I. **All is one.** Belief in absolute unity is essential to Buddhism. Unity is foundational; diversity is derivative.

One does not learn from the Buddha; one becomes the Buddha. The balancing of opposites is the highest goal in life. Compassion and cruelty, good and evil, life and death, and God and the devil must be balanced. There is no virtue in the victory of one opposite over another. To insist on the triumph of one over another is to destroy unity. There is no such thing as individuality; there is only progress and potentiality in one reality.

II. **Four Noble Truths**

   i.   **Truth of suffering.** The first law is that everyone suffers. This concept is called (in the Pali liturgical language) *dukkha,* which translates as "suffering," "anguish," "pain," or "unsatisfactoriness." According to tradition, Buddha said, "I have taught one thing and one thing only: *dukkha* and the cessation of *dukkha.*"

   ii.   **Cause of suffering.** The cause of all suffering is desire. The Pali word *tanha* conveys the idea of "grasping," "thirst, " "longing," "craving" "desire," or "attachment" and is associated with desiring things that cannot satisfy us fully. It is not mere desire but an unhealthy craving for impermanent things and an incessant thirst for self-gratification. Trying to grasp things that we do not have for ourselves leads to suffering, especially when we do not receive what we desire. Our minds are filled with pain when things do not conform to our expectations.

iii. **End of suffering.** Suffering (*dukkha*) will cease only when we experience the cessation of *tanha*. When a person ceases from desire, then he becomes one with all. Deliverance from suffering is attainable not merely by desiring to be free from suffering but by embracing the fact that "suffering is."

iv. **Freedom from suffering.** Ultimate freedom from suffering is achieved by following Buddha's eightfold path. The eightfold path is a series of moral, mental, and wisdom principles we must learn to put into practice. They include the application of right understanding, right thought, right speech, right action, right liveliness, right effort, right mindfulness, and right concentration.

III. **Cycle of life.** Like Hindu teachers before him, the Buddha advanced the idea of karma: "For every event that occurs, there will follow another event whose existence was caused by the first, and this second event will be pleasant or unpleasant according as its cause was skillful or unskillful." If everything is cause and effect in regard to our actions, and all is one in the universe, then the result of our actions will be our reincarnation or rebirth (Pali *samsara*) in the one reality in some form or another. Freedom from the cycle of rebirth is called *nirvana,* and it is attained by reaching enlightenment.

Why do people believe this form of false teaching?

In a world of division and strife, the idea of being one with everything is powerful. The idea of absolute unity offers a therapeutic benefit to the healing of minds and spirits burdened with suffering. Buddhism holds out a way to overcome enslavement to materialism and dissension. The introduction of many Eastern religious ideas in various health and fitness programs as well as in popular culture has fueled the spread of Buddhism in the Western world.

How does it hold up against biblical Christianity?

I. **Creator-creature distinction.** The philosophical problem of unity and diversity finds its solution in the biblical Creator-creature distinction. Scripture does not view all diversity as undesirable. Distinguishing between the Creator and the creature is essential for a right understanding of the world. God is not His creation, and we are not Him. God is absolute, eternal, and personal. In our fallen state, we blur and suppress the distinction between God and man (Rom. 1:22–23, 25, 28). The triune God—who is in Himself eternal unity and diversity, being one in essence and three in person—has created a temporal world of unity and diversity. God created mankind as distinct from the rest of creation. He created the plants, trees, fish, birds, and animals, "each according to its kind" (Gen. 1:11–12, 21, 24–25). God has woven diversity into the fabric of the unity of His creation. Though each person shares in common the fact that he or she is made in the image of God, is descended from Adam and Eve, fallen in Adam, and under the wrath and curse of God apart from Christ, God has created each of us to be individually distinct from another (Ps. 139:13–14).

II. **Suffering and desire.** Desire for that which is impermanent is not, in and of itself, evil. We were created to desire both what is permanent—God and that which is good in the sight of God—and what is impermanent on this side of glory—good health, material success, etc. The problem is not the act of desire but many of the intentions behind our desires and many of the objects of our desire since the fall (Jer. 2:13; James 1:14–15). Contrary to Buddhism, the Bible reveals that evil desire must be put to death and replaced with a desire for that which is better—namely, Christ. Jesus came to permanently satisfy the thirsty soul with the living water that He freely gives by His grace (John 4:10–11; 7:38; Rev. 7:17). Jesus thirsted on the cross, under the wrath of God, to atone for our evil desires, so that we would never thirst again (John 19:28). In union with Christ, we are enabled to put evil desires to death and to desire what is good, right, and true (Rom. 6:12–14; Col. 3:5).

III. **Eternal punishment and eternal life.** Scripture teaches the principle of reaping and sowing (Gal. 6:7–8) rather than the idea of karma and reincarnation. Instead of teaching a cyclical view of reality, Scripture reveals that Christ will come again to consummate all things and bring human history to a close. We will all be judged according to what we have done in the body (2 Cor. 5:10). Unbelievers will suffer eternal punishment. Those who believe in Christ will inherit eternal life (John 3:18). God does not simply overlook the believer's evil deeds. Jesus took the wrath we deserve on Himself, as our substitute, by taking our sin on Himself (1 Peter 2:24).

How can I share the gospel with those who hold to this false teaching?

I. **Focus on the Redeemer who conquers all evil.** Meditation and enlightenment can never overcome what is evil in this fallen world. Buddhism refuses to acknowledge that evil is a reality that must be conquered. Emphasize what Scripture teaches about the Son of God coming into the world in order to conquer Satan, sin, and death (Gen. 3:15; Matt. 1:21; 1 Cor. 15:26; 1 John 3:8). Explain how the Son of God came into the world to deal with the problem of our personal sin at the cross (Matt 1:21; 2 Cor. 5:21; 1 John 1:9). Help Buddhists ask the ultimate questions about God, the guilt of their own sin, and the judgment to come. Highlight the teaching of Scripture about the forgiveness of sin in the death of Jesus (Acts 2:38; 5:31; Eph. 1:7; Col. 1:14; Heb. 9:22).

II. **Focus on the biblical teaching about the renewal of all things.** Reincarnation is a counterfeit to the biblical plan of salvation. When witnessing to a Buddhist, explain that Jesus doesn't simply redeem individuals. He died and rose to secure "new heavens and a new earth in which righteousness dwells" (2 Peter 3:13). God's cosmic plan of redemption is the solution to the problem of suffering in this life. The whole of creation, which God has subjected to futility because of our sin, will be restored by Christ on the last day (Acts 3:20–21; Rom. 8:18–22; Heb. 1:10–12; 2:5–9).

—

DUKKHA

Dukkha is a central concept in Buddhist teaching. It translates roughly as "suffering" or "pain," and it refers to anything that is uncomfortable, unpleasant, or unsatisfactory about the human condition. Understanding the nature of dukkha and learning how to alleviate it are of pivotal importance in Buddhism. The Four Noble Truths teach that suffering is caused by desire and alleviated through the cessation of desire. The cessation of desire, if achieved, can lead to a state called *nirvana,* which is marked by release from the cycle of reincarnation and is often conceived of as the snuffing out of one's personal existence.

DALAI
LAMA

The Dalai Lama is the spiritual leader of the Gelug branch of Tibetan Buddhism. *Dalai Lama* is a title, meaning roughly "big guru" or "ocean of wisdom." The Dalai Lama is considered to be the reincarnation of the previous title holder; upon the Dalai Lama's death, a search commences for his successor. The current title holder is Tenzin Gyatso (1935–), the fourteenth Dalai Lama. In 1951, the People's Republic of China occupied Tibet, and in 1959, an uprising prompted the Dalai Lama to flee to India, where he established the Tibetan Government in Exile. He is recognized internationally as a teacher, peace advocate, and proponent of religious harmony.

HINDUISM

What is Hinduism?

The religion known as Hinduism is actually a collection of several associated religious traditions that originated in ancient India. The third-largest religion in the world, Hinduism today has more than nine hundred million adherents. Like Buddhism, Hinduism is a *monistic* religion, which means that it sees all reality as ultimately one. Hindus seek oneness with the Ultimate Reality or Spirit *(Brahman)*. Unlike Buddhism, modern Hinduism tends toward henotheism. Henotheism is the worship of one supreme god, together with manifestations (i.e., avatars) of that god in a plurality of gods and goddesses.[29] In Hinduism, religion and society are inseparably connected in a caste system—a fixed social hierarchy. There are four main branches of Hinduism: Vaishnavism, Shaivism, Shaktism, and Smartism. However, Hinduism is an incredibly large and diverse religion, and there is much variety of belief and practice within each of its main branches.

When did it begin?

The word *Hindu* refers to the land and inhabitants surrounding the Indus River. References to this region in Hindu scriptures have led scholars to conclude that northern India was the birthplace of Hinduism. The absence of a single founding figure distinguishes Hinduism from almost every other world religion. While Hinduism has a set of sacred writings, they are not viewed as divine revelation in the same way that Christians view the Bible as divine revelation or in the way Muslims affirm that the Qur'an is divine revelation. Hinduism originated between 2000 and 1500 BC, making it one of the world's oldest religions. Hindu beliefs and practices originally spread and were passed down via oral tradition. The earliest body of Hindu sacred writings is the Vedas—from a Sanskrit word meaning "knowledge" or "wisdom"—which take the form of ancient hymns. The Vedas comprise four books—the Rig-Veda, Sama-Veda, Yajur-Veda, and Atharva-Veda. The Rig-Veda is the most ancient of the Vedas. The concluding portions of the Vedas, known as the Upanishads, cover philosophical topics and are the foundational texts for most Hindu spiritual study. The most well-known Hindu text is the *Bhagavad Gita*, which is part of the ancient Hindu epic *Mahabharata*. The *Bhagavad Gita* contains the essence of Hindu devotional teaching.

Who are the key figures?

The eighth-century philosopher Adi Shankara unified Hinduism through a careful study of the *Vedas* and *Upanishads*. He is author of the Hindu saying "*Atman* is *Brahman*," which encapsulates the idea that each individual soul (*atman*) is finally one with the Ultimate Spirit (*Brahman*).

The nineteenth-century monk Swami Vivekananda

represented Hinduism at the World Parliament of Religions in Chicago in 1893. He brought about significant reform in the caste system.

Mohandas Gandhi is arguably the most well-known Hindu to modern people. He is renowned for his teaching on nonviolent civil disobedience to achieve social and political reform in India in the early to mid-twentieth century.

Among popular figures, the Beatles' George Harrison was a Hindu convert, as are actress Julia Roberts and actor Russell Brand.

What are the main beliefs?

I.   **One and many gods.** Hindus believe in one impersonal god or Ultimate Reality—Brahman—while affirming the existence of a plurality of gods and goddesses. There are three chief manifestations of Brahman—Brahma, Vishnu, and Shiva—from whom all other gods and goddesses are incarnate manifestations. Brahma, the creator god, is largely ignored in modern Hinduism, while Vishnu, the preserving god, and Shiva, the destroying god, have many worshipers. Many Hindus also render their primary devotion not to Vishnu or Shiva but to Shakti, a feminine representative of Brahman that manifests herself as many different goddesses. For all practical purposes, popular Hindu devotion identifies Vishnu, Shiva, or Shakti as Brahman depending on the Hindu tradition followed. All Hindus believe that Brahman manifests itself in a multitude of avatars—earthly incarnations of gods and goddesses. It has often been said that there are 330 million gods and goddesses (avatars) in Hinduism. This number should not be taken literally but "is an exaggeration meant to emphasize the multitude of the gods."[30]

II. **Dharma.** The concept of *dharma* is central to Hinduism. Although it is difficult to translate, *dharma* represents Hindu duty, conduct, law, order, religion, virtue, justice, and morality. It plays a significant role in the Indian caste system. Each caste has its own rules and regulations by which members must abide. *Dharma* is related to *karma* and the cycle of rebirth or reincarnation, as faithful observance of particular duties is necessary for moving into a higher caste in the next life. A person may not move out of the caste, essentially one's social class, into which he was born during his lifetime.

III. **Karma.** The doctrine of *karma* is the backbone of the religious and social system of Hinduism.[31] *Karma* says that whatever someone has—whether physical appearance, financial status, personality, health, or sorrow—is a result of his past life. One goes through the cycle of reincarnation based on his *dharma* in a previous life. If someone gives himself to vice and moral degeneration, he will not be destroyed or cease to exist. Rather, he will continue in the cycle of reincarnation—as long as necessary—until his soul reaches nirvana and he becomes one with the Ultimate Reality. If someone lives a life of bad *dharma*, he will be reborn in a lower caste or as a lower life form in the next cycle.

Why do people believe this form of false teaching?

The spread of Hinduism is due in large part to its antiquity and to its comprehensiveness. Its ideology encompasses the totality of an individual's familial, social, and religious life, making departure difficult and costly. The Brahmins (priests and teachers of the highest caste) exercise power over the lives of those in lower castes, confining them in the system. In the Western world, elements of Hinduism have spread through the popularity of yoga in gyms and exercise programs. Western popular culture has also long been fascinated by Eastern religions such as Hinduism. For instance, the Beatles popularized Hindu ideas through their travels to India and their advocacy of Hindu-influenced Transcendental Meditation during the 1960s.

How does it hold up against biblical Christianity?

I. **Only one God.** Contrary to Hinduism, the Bible reveals that there is only one true and living God. This true God is a personal being. He does not change (Mal. 3:6). The one God subsists in three persons—the Father, Son, and Holy Spirit—who are each fully divine and yet distinct from one another according to each one's unique personal property. The Son is not an avatar of the Father, and the Father did not become the incarnate Son. Rather, the person of the Son of God united a sinless human nature to His eternal divine nature, thereby becoming the God-man. The Father, Son, and Spirit eternally exist as the one true God. When the New Testament speaks of the members of the Godhead, it places them side by side, distinguishing them according to their personal properties while maintaining that they are identical in terms of the one divine essence (1 Cor. 8:6; 12:4–6; 2 Cor. 13:14; 2 Thess. 2:13–14; 1 Peter 1:2; 1 John 5:4–6; Rev. 1:4–6).

II. **Law and grace.** The Bible contains prescriptive duties, laws, rituals, and principles of virtue, justice, and morality. In His law, God reveals His will for the conduct of His people. However, no one is saved by attempting to keep the law. All people, except Christ, are fallen and unable to please God by nature (Rom. 3:10–20; 5:12–21) and are under God's wrath and curse (Gal. 3:13). In Adam, we are dead in sin and depravity and need a salvation from outside ourselves. God initiates, procures, and provides salvation entirely by His grace. There is no grace in Hindu teaching. People are rewarded or punished exclusively on the basis of good or bad *dharma*. According to Scripture, God redeems a people for Himself based on the merit of Jesus Christ, the eternal Son of God, who—as our representative—kept the law perfectly and took the punishment we deserve. In Christ, God forgives, accepts, and reconciles believers to Himself (1 Cor. 1:30).

III. **Death, judgment, and salvation.** Death is a result of the sin of Adam. God will judge men for what they have done in this life. Apart from grace, we are subject to the eternal wrath of God because of sin (Rom. 1:18; Eph. 5:6; Col. 3:5–6; Rev. 19:15). Only those who trust in Christ will gain eternal life (John 3:16–18). As the writer of Hebrews explains, "It is appointed for man to die once, and after that comes judgment, so Christ, having been offered once to bear the sins of many, will appear a second time, not to deal with sin but to save those who are eagerly waiting for him" (9:27–28).

How can I share the gospel with those who hold to this false teaching?

I. **Focus on sin and judgment.** When witnessing to Hindus, explain that sin is not, first and foremost, a violation of social norms or an offense against one's caste. Sin is primarily an offense against God (Gen. 39:9; Ps. 51:4). Since Hindus typically think of punishment for sin in terms of social degradation and not as justice incurred for a personal offense against the Creator, it is vital to help them think properly about the eternal ramifications of sinning against the eternal

"

FOR ALL HAVE
SINNED AND FALL
SHORT OF THE
GLORY OF GOD,
AND ARE JUSTIFIED
BY HIS GRACE AS A
GIFT, THROUGH THE
REDEMPTION THAT
IS IN CHRIST JESUS.

ROMANS 3:23–24

God. Scripture is full of references to eternal death and judgment on sin (Gen. 2:17; Ps. 5:5; 11:5; 50:21; 94:10; Rom. 1:18; 2:3; 6:21, 23; Gal. 3:10; Eph. 2:3).

II. **Focus on forgiveness of sins in Christ.** Hindus—especially those in lower castes—spend their lives seeking to work their way out of the caste system. Many are burdened with the weight of their failings. Hindus need to hear about the forgiveness that God freely gives in Christ. Jesus said, "Come to me, all who labor and are heavy laden, and I will give you rest" (Matt. 11:28). Explain that God took the punishment for our sin in the person of Jesus Christ (2 Cor. 5:21). Share God's promises of forgiveness to all who trust in Jesus alone for salvation (Ex. 34:6–7; Ps. 130:4; Jer. 31:34; Dan. 9:9; Acts 5:31; 13:38; 26:18; Rom. 4:7; Eph. 1:7; Col. 1:14).

III. **Focus on Jesus as Mediator.** Man's great need is to be reconciled to God. The Bible teaches that reconciliation happens only through the mediatorial work of Jesus Christ (2 Cor. 5:19). As God and man, Jesus bridges the gap between the infinitely holy God and sinners. Jesus died on the cross to bring us to God (1 Peter 3:18). Jesus is the Great High Priest of believers. He "always lives to make intercession for them" (Heb. 7:25). Jesus is the only Mediator. He said: "I am the way, and the truth, and the life. No one comes to the Father except through me" (John 14:6). Paul also explained, "There is one God, and there is one mediator between God and men, the man Christ Jesus" (1 Tim. 2:5).

—

BRAHMAN

Brahman is the ultimate principle or reality in Hindu theology. It is conceived of in various ways in the many different schools of Hinduism. Though Brahman is considered the source of all that is, it is not seen as a personal creator god but rather as the impersonal material or principle that underlies all reality. All that we see and experience is a temporary and changing manifestation of the eternal and unchanging reality that is Brahman. The relationship of the soul (*atman*) to Brahman is a key concept in Hinduism. In theistic schools, atman is separate from Brahman and each soul is separate from the others. However, most schools are monistic and see atman as one with or the same as Brahman. The goal, then, is to understand this truth and to become one with Brahman at death. The oneness of Brahman also informs Hindu ethics. Since all is one, each person is related to or part of every other person; therefore, human beings ought to be compassionate to others and strive for others' welfare and happiness.

—

DHARMA

Dharma is a central concept in Hindu ethics. There is no one English word that completely captures the concept of *dharma*, but it can be loosely understood as the right way of living. It has to do with how one acts in himself and also how he acts toward others, and it is often illustrated in the Hindu scriptures in stories and illustrations. The epic *Mahabharata*, for example, presents problems as having three possible solutions that are embodied by three different characters. The choices that humans make will tend toward *dharma* or its opposite, *adharma*, and these choices redound to the next life one lives in the cycle of reincarnation. Therefore, the blame for one's station in life always lies with oneself, a teaching that lies behind the poor treatment given to those in lower castes in India.

ISLAM

What is Islam?

Islam is the second-largest religion in the world. Today, an estimated 1.3 billion people profess to be Muslims—that is, followers of the religion of Islam. Of these, nearly 1 billion reside in the Middle East, North Africa, and Southeast Asia. Islam is a monotheistic religion, requiring submission to the one God, Allah, and to everything Allah revealed through the prophet Muhammad. The two major authoritative texts in Islam are the Qur'an and the *hadith*. The Qur'an is claimed to be the revelation of Allah to Muhammad. The *hadith* are the oral traditions of Muhammad's teaching and practice as passed down in the Muslim community and set to writing a few centuries later. The Five Pillars of Islam structure the essence of Islamic belief and practice. There are two major branches of Islam: the Sunnis and the Shiites, and there is also a large mystical tradition, the Sufis. The Nation of Islam, an African American political and religious movement, has brought an awareness of Islam to many Americans. However, this movement is a modern Western ethnocentric religion that is not recognized by orthodox Muslims as an authentic Islamic tradition.

When did it begin?

Muhammad is the founder of Islam. He was born in AD 570 in Mecca (a city in the western Arabian Peninsula).[32] His father died before his birth. His mother died when he was six. Muhammad went to live with his grandfather Abd al-Muttalib. When he was eight, Muhammad's grandfather died. Muhammad then went to live with his uncle Abu Talib, a caravan tradesman. Abu Talib took Muhammad on many of his travels.

At age twenty-five, Muhammad married Khadija, a wealthy traveling merchant. Khadija had been raised by

Ebionite Christians. The Ebionites were a mystical Jewish sect of Christianity that denied the deity of Christ. Scholars believe that Muhammad learned his inaccurate versions of biblical accounts on his travels with Abu Talib and Khadija.

Muhammad said the angel Gabriel visited him in Mecca in 610, which began a twenty-three-year period during which Muhammad claimed to receive the revelation of the Qur'an. Traditionally, eighty-six *suras* (chapters) of the Qur'an are said to have been revealed while Muhammad lived in Mecca, while the remaining twenty-eight were revealed in the city of Medina.

The first two people to accept Muhammad's message were his wife, Khadija, and his cousin, Ali ibn Abi Talib. The first convert outside of Muhammad's family was Abu Bakr, a traveling merchant. During his stay in Mecca, Muhammad began calling the polytheistic citizens to repent and submit to Allah, the one true God. After years of rejection, persecution, and warfare, Muhammad journeyed to Medina (then known as Yathrib) in 622. This event, called the *Hijrah*, marks the beginning of the Islamic calendar. The message of Islam found greater acceptance in Medina; the Muslim community there grew, and Muhammad became the leader of the city. Eventually, Muhammad was able to amass an army large enough to capture Mecca, which he purged of polytheism. Mecca is today one of the holiest cities in Islam.

Upon Muhammad's death in 632, Abu Bakr became the first caliph (the religious and political leader of the Islamic state), although many Muslims believed the caliph should have been a relative of Muhammad, specifically his cousin Ali. Abu Bakr carried on the Islamic religion until his death. Caliphs Umar Ibn al-Khattab, Uthman ibn Affan, and Muhammad's cousin Ali succeeded Abu Bakr, in that order. After Ali's death, disagreements within the Muslim community over who could be caliph continued to grow, with the Shiites eventually breaking with the majority of Muslims—the Sunnis—over the Shiite belief that the caliph had to be from Muhammad's family.

Who are the key figures?

Over its long history, Islam has produced a multitude of influential rulers, scholars, philosophers, authors, athletes, businessmen, scientists, and teachers. Muslim mathematicians and philosophers have played important roles in the development of disciplines such as algebra and in the recovery of Aristotle's thought in the West during the late medieval period. Islamic empires conquered much of the Christian East.

Today, the most well-known Islamic political figures are King Abdullah of Jordan; King Salman of Saudi Arabia; Ayatollah Ali Khamenei, the supreme leader of Iran; and Mohammed VI, king of Morocco.

Before becoming a Sunni Muslim, Malcom X helped raise awareness of the Nation of Islam in American culture. Louis Farrakhan is currently the leader of the Nation of Islam, a ethnocentric sect viewed as heretical by orthodox Muslims.

Muhammad Ali, Mike Tyson, and Kareem Abdul-Jabbar are among the famous Muslim athletes of recent decades.

What are the main beliefs?

I.   **Revelation and interpretation.** Although all Muslims profess belief in the Qur'an, considerable diversity of belief and practice exists among the various branches

of Islam. Sunni Muslims, who make up the vast majority of the worldwide Muslim community, rely heavily
on legal scholars to settle disputes over the teaching
of the Qur'an. These lawyers, in the development of
Islamic law or *sharia*, seek to reconcile the differences
between the teaching of the Qur'an and the *hadith* by
means of consensus and analogy. Shiite Muslims, who
make up the second-largest group of Muslims worldwide, believe that the true successor to Muhammad
as leader of all Muslims comes from the family of Ali.
(Sunnis believe that Muhammad's successor can come
from the broader Islamic community.) The Shiites
also have their own collections of *hadith*, consisting
only of traditions that they trace back to Ali. Disputes
within Shiite Islam are settled by appointed imams
whose decisions are considered binding. The Sufis
believe in a spiritual, nonliteral interpretation of the
Qur'an and engage in mystical practices. One of the
most famous of these practices is the whirling dance
that is particularly associated with the Mevlevi Order
of Sufis (the Whirling Dervishes).

Though it professes to be the authoritative revelation of the one true God, the Qur'an includes a number of historically and theologically inaccurate accounts of biblical figures. For instance, the Qur'an teaches that Abraham offered up Ishmael rather than Isaac. The Qur'an also teaches that Isa ibn Maryam (Jesus, the son of Mary) was merely a miracle-working prophet of Allah. Additionally, the Qur'an denies the deity and atoning death of Jesus. It states, "They slew him not nor crucified him, but it appeared so unto them . . . they slew him not for certain. But Allah took him up unto Himself" (Surah 4:157–58).[33]

II. **Devotion.** The Five Pillars of Islam encapsulate the essential religious beliefs and practices of Islam. They are as follows:

   i. **Confession of faith.** The first pillar of Islam is the *shahada*—profession of belief. First, it requires the confession of "no god but Allah." Second, it requires acceptance of "Muhammad as the messenger of Allah." In Islamic belief, Muhammad is the last and greatest prophet of Allah.

ii. **Prayers.** The second pillar of Islam is *salat*—daily prayers. Muslims are expected to pray five times a day—at dawn, at noon, in the afternoon, at sunset, and at night. This practice is evidence of their submission and allegiance to Allah.

iii. **Giving.** The third pillar is *zakat*—regular giving. Muslims are required to give approximately 2.5 percent of their wealth to religious officials of an Islamic state or to the local mosque. This practice supports the needs of the community, the relief of poverty, the upkeep of religious meeting places, and the propagation of the faith.

iv. **Fasting.** The fourth pillar of Islam is *sawm*— fasting during Ramadan, the ninth month of the Islamic lunar calendar. From sunup to sundown, Muslims must abstain from eating, drinking, and sexual activity. This practice is a sign of purification through bodily sacrifice to Allah. Muhammad claimed to have had his visions during Ramadan.

v. **Pilgrimage.** The fifth pillar of Islam is the *hajj*—a pilgrimage to Mecca. Everyone who has the financial means and physical ability is required to make a trip to Mecca at least once in his life. There are a number of ritual practices that Muslims must do on their pilgrimage. One of the most important is walking counterclockwise around the Kaaba (a sacred shrine in Mecca that Muslims consider the holiest spot on earth) seven times.

III. **Redemption.** While the Qur'an encourages Muslims to turn to Allah for mercy, it teaches that redemption is based on the freedom of Allah's will. A person can atone for his sins by devotion to Allah, repentance, and good works. Allah is free to extend or withhold mercy as he likes, meaning he can set aside his love and justice when making a decision about a person's ultimate destiny. Every single person will either end up in paradise (the Islamic concept of heaven) or in hell. However, some *hadith* seem to teach that ultimately Allah will bring the people in hell into paradise. Muhammad declared, "Allah will bring out people from the Fire and admit them into Paradise" (Sahih Muslim 1:368).

Why do people believe this form of false teaching?

One of the three major monotheistic religions that trace themselves back to Abraham, Islam has some superficial resemblances to Judaism and Christianity. Biblical accounts in the Qur'an—though historically inaccurate—make Islam a compelling counterfeit of the Christian religion. Many have been attracted to the ethical and ritualistic aspects of Islam. Additionally, the sociopolitical nature of Islam ensures its spread to every facet of the lives of its members, giving people who are looking for order and structure in their lives something to latch onto.

How does it hold up against biblical Christianity?

I.   **Revelation.** In contrast to Islam, Christianity maintains that the triune God has revealed Himself fully and finally through His prophets and Apostles in the Old and New Testaments. The Holy Spirit superintended the revelation of God's salvation in Christ through many men over a period of 1,500 years (Heb. 1:1–2; 1 Peter 1:10–12; 2 Peter 1:21). God has fully revealed Himself in His Son. Jesus is not only the great Prophet; He is God in the flesh (John 1:1, 14; Rom. 9:5; 1 Tim. 3:16). The overarching message of Scripture is the suffering of Christ and His subsequent glory (Luke 24:25–26, 44–47; 1 Peter 1:10–12). All special revelation has ceased after the ministry of Jesus and the Apostles (Heb. 1:2; Rev. 22:18–19).

II. **Devotion.** Scripture stresses the importance of confession of faith in God and Christ (Matt. 16:16; John 3:16–18; Rom. 10:9–10). The Bible encourages believers to be fervent in prayer (1 Thess. 5:17; James 5:16) and faithful in giving (1 Cor. 16:1; Gal. 6:6). However, religious devotion is an act of gratitude for the redemption that we have in Christ by grace. Christianity does not encourage pilgrimage to any physical building. The old covenant temple served its purpose in redemptive history. The physical temple was a type of Christ, and

"

LONG AGO, AT
MANY TIMES AND
IN MANY WAYS,
GOD SPOKE TO OUR
FATHERS BY THE
PROPHETS, BUT IN
THESE LAST DAYS
HE HAS SPOKEN TO
US BY HIS SON.

HEBREWS 1:1–2

His church—His people—in the new covenant era are His temple (John 2:19–22; 4:21; 1 Cor. 6:19; 1 Peter 2:4–5).

III. **Redemption.** The Bible teaches that all men are born dead in sin (Eph. 2:1–4). No amount of good works can save us. No number of religious acts can give someone a right standing before God. Scripture teaches that Jesus, the eternal Son of God, died on the cross to atone for the sins of His people and to propitiate the wrath of God for His people (1 John 1:8–2:2). Jesus represents His people before God on the basis of His sinless life, atoning death, and continual intercession (2 Cor. 5:21; Heb. 7:25). We are saved by faith in Christ, not by our works (Rom. 4:1–8; Eph. 2:8–9). Though God freely chooses to show mercy to some and not to others (Ex. 33:19; Rom. 9:15), He does not annul His love or justice to do so. Rather, at the cross, God upholds His justice by punishing His Son in the place of His people and displays His love by forgiving them and reconciling them to Himself (Rom. 3:26).

How can I share the gospel with those who hold to this false teaching?

I. **Focus on the unity of Scripture.** Since the Qur'an incorporates portions of the Old and New Testaments, we must help Muslims see the internal unity and coherence of the Bible. The Old and New Testaments center on the person and saving work of Jesus. As He walked with His disciples on the road to Emmaus, Jesus "interpreted to them in all the Scriptures the things concerning himself" (Luke 24:27). The message of the Old Testament is the same as that of the New Testament—namely, that God saves sinners by grace through Christ crucified and risen (John 5:46; 8:58; Gal. 3:8).

II. **Focus on the biblical teaching about the immanence of God.** According to Islam, Allah is utterly and exclusively transcendent and nonrelational. Therefore, it is vital for us to stress the biblical truth about the immanence or nearness of the triune God when witnessing to Muslims. Scripture teaches that God is both transcendent and immanent (Isa. 55:8; 64:1). In the person of Jesus, God came into the world to accomplish redemption (John 1:1, 14). God the Holy Spirit works directly in creation in both revelation and regeneration. God drew near to His prophets in redemptive history in order to give the revelation of Himself to His people (2 Peter 1:21). The Spirit regenerates the hearts of His people, enabling them to believe and commune with God (John 3:5–6; Titus 3:5).

III. **Focus on atonement and assurance.** The biblical teaching about the atoning sacrifice of Jesus is the most important thing that we can share with Muslims. God freely provides an atoning sacrifice for sins in the sacrificial death of Jesus (John 1:29, 36). Since Jesus' death on the cross is an efficacious sacrifice for all those for whom He died, nothing can separate believers from God (Rom. 8:35–39). Muslims follow a works-based religion and thus live with uncertainty whether Allah will admit them to paradise. No such uncertainty exists in the message of the gospel (John 17:3; Rom. 8:1; 1 John 5:13).

622

Six twenty-two is the year of the *Hijrah*, the journey of Muhammad from Mecca to Medina (then known as Yathrib). This event marks the beginning of the Islamic calendar. Muhammad had urged the inhabitants of Mecca to renounce their paganism and return to Islam, which he said was their original religion, but they reacted with hostility.

Medina, however, was receptive, as residents of the city came to Muhammad to learn about Islam and pledged to receive him as a prophet. Muhammad sent followers to preach Islam, after which the city invited Muhammad to come and reconcile its warring tribes. He accepted their invitation and migrated in 622 to Medina, which at the time was home to various tribes of Jews and pagan Arabs. Muhammad enacted the Constitution of Medina to end the conflict and unite the tribes. Though the Jews were guaranteed religious freedom, they were eventually expelled or slaughtered. Muhammad solidified his position through a series of battles with Mecca before returning to capture the city in 630.

—

JIHAD

Jihad, meaning "struggle" or "striving," is an important concept in Islam. In general, it has to do with attempts by the Muslim to conform his life to the principles of Allah as found in the Qur'an and the *hadith*. It is often equated with armed conflict today, especially in connection with Islamist terrorist groups, but its meaning is debated among Islamic scholars. Some think the primary reference is internal, as in the war against one's evil inclinations; some think the primary reference is external but limited to defensive battles; and some think the primary reference is to offensive war against unbelievers. One who engages in *jihad* is called a *mujahid* (pl. *mujahideen*), a term that became well known as a description of fighters in Afghanistan.

NEW AGE SPIRITUALITY

What is New Age spirituality?

New Age spirituality is an umbrella term that describes a contemporary religious movement, not an organized religion. Proponents of the movement encourage striving to reach one's full potential through an eclectic mixture of concepts and practices drawn from Eastern mysticism, Hinduism, Buddhism, metaphysics, naturalism, astrology, occultism, and science fiction. In its various forms, New Age spirituality is both *monistic* (believing that all reality is ultimately one) and *pantheistic* (believing that everything is divine). Unlike organized religions, New Age spirituality has no founding figure, structured leadership, official head-quarters, or authoritative writings that are accepted by all proponents. New Age spirituality has held considerable social sway over Western culture over the past three decades. An estimated one in three Americans accepts various elements of New Age ideology.

When did it begin?

References to the "New Age" come from the world of astrology. Roughly every 2,100 years, proponents argue, we enter a new "astrological age" that corresponds to one of the twelve signs of the zodiac. The exact date of the transition is disputed, but most astrologers maintain that we transitioned from the Age of Pisces to the Age of Aquarius sometime in the twentieth century.

The contemporary New Age movement originated in the late 1960s and early 1970s, concurrent with the hippie counterculture movement. The Beatles popularized Eastern mysticism and monistic religion in mainstream America after returning in 1965 from a trip to India, where they practiced Transcendental Meditation with the Indian guru

Maharishi Mahesh Yogi. The 1967 musical *Hair* promoted the astrological elements of the New Age movement with its catchy opening number, which asserted, "This is the dawning of the Age of Aquarius." In 1969, the promoters of the music festival Woodstock publicized it as "an Aquarian exposition: 3 Days of Peace and Love."

Who are the key figures?

Academy Award–winning actress Shirley MacLaine promoted the New Age ideas of reincarnation and past life experiences in her 1984 book *Out on a Limb*. In 1989, Deepak Chopra published his book *Quantum Healing,* which claims to integrate modern scientific concepts into an Eastern mystical framework with the goal of healing the body. Eckhart Tolle, author of *The Power of Now* and *A New Earth,* is among the most well-known proponents of the New Age movement today. In a 2008 article, *The New York Times* called Tolle "the most popular spiritual author in [the United States]."[34] Prominent media personality Oprah Winfrey continues to be one of the most vocal proponents of New Age ideology.

What are the main beliefs?

It is nearly impossible to set out any systematic doctrine associated with the New Age movement, since it borrows from so many religious and esoteric traditions. However, New Age proponents hold in common several broad ideas:

I. **Cosmological determination.** According to astrologers, the movement of stars and other heavenly bodies determines cultural and societal—as well as individual—development. Accordingly, humanity has moved out of the Age of Pisces, in which we sought to discover our identity and existence, into the Age of Aquarius, in which we seek total peace and unity. Having collectively moved into a new era, we are to embrace the cultural changes that coincide with the current astrological age. This shift has already had an impact on every person and will continue to do so. All that we learned from our parents, and all that our parents learned from their parents, was a result of the influence of the Piscean age and must now be largely abandoned. In the Age of Aquarius, we must learn to

"

THEY EXCHANGED
THE TRUTH ABOUT
GOD FOR A LIE
AND WORSHIPED
AND SERVED
THE CREATURE
RATHER THAN THE
CREATOR, WHO IS
BLESSED FOREVER!
AMEN.

ROMANS 1:25

accept ourselves as people who do not need to believe in anything that lies outside ourselves. All that is in us and all that is in the universe is God; therefore, to gain unity and balance with God, we must seek to embrace what is happening in this present Aquarian age as the divine expresses itself in us and in others. This form of pantheism attributes to the created order something that belongs exclusively to the eternal sovereignty of God.

II. **Monistic energy.** Proponents of the New Age movement believe that God and the universe are one in substance. The New Age movement rejects biblical monotheism in favor of monism or pantheism. Proponents of the New Age believe that there is divine energy inherent in every part of the universe. In order to regain energy or power from the universe, one must attain harmony with every aspect of the universe. In the New Age movement, the means of achieving harmony and regaining personal power are exceedingly diverse. To achieve this unity, practitioners encourage the use of ancient and modern forms of meditation, seances, divination, numerology, and incantation. Many New Age proponents believe that practicing yoga will enable them to advance in the New Age quest for balance and harmony.

III. **Self-deification.** The New Age movement teaches that we have everything in ourselves necessary to achieve fulfillment. The self is the highest good. We exist to guide ourselves, heal ourselves, and fulfill our own destinies. Many who embrace New Age practices believe in karma and reincarnation. As in Hinduism, the ultimate goal in the New Age movement is to achieve oneness with the divine. Adherents of New Age spirituality reject the biblical doctrines of the fall, the sinfulness and depravity of man, the need for an atoning sacrifice, and the need for a mediator between God and man.

Why do people believe this form of false teaching?

While the New Age movement rejects the idea that mankind is different from other parts of the created order, it is an excellent example of what happens when people consistently embrace the supremacy and autonomy of man. The idea that we have the power in ourselves to progress, achieve harmony with the universe, and guide our own destiny is supremely attractive to fallen men and women who want peace and freedom but not on God's terms.

How does it hold up against biblical Christianity?

I. **Divine sovereignty.** Contrary to the New Age movement, Scripture teaches that the living God works out His eternal, sovereign decree in the works of creation and providence. The Creator maintains His sovereignty, and the creation maintains its dependence on Him. Herman Bavinck explained, "The theism of Scripture posits a connection between God and the world, simultaneously maintains the absolute sovereignty of God and the complete dependence of his creatures, thus avoiding both the error of pantheism and that of Deism."[35] The triune God is sovereign over all His creatures and all their actions (Judg. 14:3–4;

Ps. 115:3; Dan. 4:34–35). There is nothing that lies outside His eternal plan. God has not invested in creation the ultimate power to determine the course of social and cultural ideologies. Neither is He part of the created world. God lies outside time and space, dwelling in eternity (Isa. 57:15).

II. **Divine power.** Scripture teaches that God is infinite in power. The triune God upholds the world by the word of His power (Heb. 1:3). All creation is utterly dependent on God for all things (Acts 17:25). God has not invested an independent power into creation. Rather, He has made known His power through the preaching of the cross (1 Cor. 1:18, 24). In the message of Christ crucified, God exhibits and imparts His saving power to those who believe (Rom. 1:16). The unity that we desire with God and creation is achieved only through the saving work of Jesus. By His death on the cross, Jesus unites believers to God and to other believers (Eph. 2:14).

III. **Divine purpose.** The Bible reveals that God is the highest good. God created man to glorify Him by

"

THE MOST
CREATIVE ACT YOU
WILL EVER UNDERTAKE
IS THE ACT OF
CREATING YOURSELF.

DEEPAK CHOPRA

fulfilling His holy purpose in the world. When God created the world, He made every living thing "according to its kind" (Gen. 1:11, 12, 21, 25; 6:20). God created man after His own image—distinct from other living things in the universe (Gen. 1:26). He commissioned man to rule over the rest of creation (Gen. 1:26; Ps. 8:6–8). After the fall, God fulfilled this creational mandate through the death and resurrection of Christ (Heb. 2:5–9). By His atoning death on the cross, Jesus secured the new creation. He now sits at the right hand of God as the head of a redeemed humanity. On judgment day, those who have been redeemed by Christ will rule with Christ, judging the unbelieving nations (Rev. 2:26) and the fallen angels (1 Cor. 6:3). Redeemed humanity will never become divine. There will always be a distinction between the Creator and the creature.

How can I share the gospel with those who hold to this false teaching?

I. **Focus on the being of God.** Proponents of New Age spirituality need to understand the biblical teaching on the nature and attributes of God. God is the self-existent and self-sustaining source of all life. While many who are involved in New Age practices speak of God in general terms, they do not know Him as the infinite and eternal God of Scripture. Since New Age ideology is monistic and pantheistic at its core, it is vital that adherents have Christian theism explained to them from Scripture. The triune God is transcendent. Man is finite. Explain that the God of Scripture is spirit (John 4:24), infinite, eternal, and unchangeable in all His divine perfections (Ex. 34:6; Ps. 86:5, 15; Jonah 4:2).

II. **Focus on the Creator-creature distinction.** When witnessing to those who hold to New Age ideology, it is vital to explain the doctrine of creation (Gen. 1; Heb. 11:3). Seek opportunities to talk about the biblical teaching on God's creation of man uniquely in His image (Gen 1:26; 2:7–9). Like all monistic religions, New Age spirituality removes the distinction between the Creator and the creature. Consider taking those to whom you are witnessing to Romans 1:18–32 in order to explain the moral responsibility that we have to God as our Creator.

III. **Focus on the need for redemption.** In all forms of New Age spirituality, individuals are seeking a peace, unity, and fulfillment that can be found only in Jesus Christ. To help rescue someone who is ensnared in New Age teaching, seek to use the law of God to reveal the sinfulness of man and our need for the atoning sacrifice of Jesus. Focus on the fall of man and the ultimate consequences of sin (Gen. 3; Rom. 6:23). Explain why we need a mediator between God and man who reconciles man to God by taking the sin and punishment man deserves because of his sin (2 Cor. 5:21; 1 Tim. 2:5) and obtaining a righteousness for His people that they could never achieve (Rom. 5:19; Phil. 3:9).

ASTROLOGICAL AGE

A n astrological age is a concept that has great significance in New Age spirituality. Each astrological age corresponds to one of the twelve signs of the zodiac; as the axis of the earth precesses, or wobbles, it very slowly shifts the direction of the sky to which it points. Over the course of about twenty-six thousand years, the earth's axis makes one full rotation. The current age is determined by the location of the sun in relation to the background stars on the vernal equinox. Astrologers differ on when the transition from the Age of Pisces to the Age of Aquarius happened because there are disagreements about the boundaries between the constellations. In New Age spirituality, the sign of the current astrological age is said to have tremendous effects on humanity that correspond to that sign, meaning that the transition from one age to another is a momentous event that can literally usher in changes for mankind.

ATHEISM AND SECULARISM

What are atheism and secularism?

Atheism and secularism are two widely influential modern philosophical worldviews. Though not organized religions, these two philosophical worldviews are inherently anti-religious. Proponents of atheism reject theism and religion. Proponents of secularism reject the presence of theism and religion in political and societal institutions. All atheists profess to be secularists; however, not all secularists profess to be atheists. An estimated 250 to 500 million people worldwide do not profess belief in any deity. This includes two hundred million to four hundred million residents of countries such as Russia and China, as well as thirty million residents of the United States.

When did they begin?

Although there have been a variety of philosophies since the fall of Adam that we may consider anti-theistic, atheism and secularism as we know them today originated in the Enlightenment in Britain and Continental Europe during the eighteenth century. Authors, scientists, and philosophers such as John Locke, Isaac Newton, Immanuel Kant, Johann Wolfgang von Goethe, Voltaire, Jean-Jacques Rousseau, and Adam Smith were leading figures of the Enlightenment, although none of these men were strict atheists but were either deists or held to unorthodox expressions of the Christian faith. The Enlightenment's emphasis on reason and individualism, over against religious tradition, supported the spread of deism, pantheism, and—eventually—atheism.

The Enlightenment in France particularly fueled atheism and secularism in the Western world. Baron Paul-Henri Thiry d'Holbach—an atheist intellectual—taught a form of mechanistic metaphysics that served as a catalyst for the modern atheism movement. D'Holbach devoted two works to the defense and propagation of atheism: *Système de la Nature* and *Le Bon Sens.* His contemporary Denis Diderot is believed to have assisted him in the production of the strongly atheistic and materialistic book *Système de la Nature.* Diderot was the first to give a modern definition of atheism, including it in his *Encyclopédie.*

With the rise of the scientific revolution, materialistic understandings of the origins of the universe became more widely accepted in the West. Accordingly, the publication of Charles Darwin's *On the Origin of the Species* in 1859 was seized upon by atheists as providing a scientific justification for their view. Darwin's work fostered secularist agendas in Western countries, primarily through Karl Marx's application of Darwin's principles to his economic and political theories. In *Das Kapital,* Marx appealed to Darwin's contributions. Although Darwin was not supportive of Marx's use of his philosophy for the propagation of political and economic socialism, the rise of secularism can be directly tied to the influence of Darwin on Marx.

After Marx, the nineteenth-century German philosopher Friedrich Nietzsche further advanced anti-theistic philosophy throughout the Western world. On numerous occasions, Nietzsche used the phrase "God is dead" to explain the effects of the Enlightenment in producing an increasing disbelief in God and subsequent secularization in Western society.

In 1927, the British philosopher Bertrand Russell gave a talk at the National Secular Society in London that was later published in 1969 under the title *Why I Am Not a Christian and Other Essays on Religion and Related Subjects.* This book had a significant effect on readers in Britain and America, further popularizing atheism and secularism. Russell helped pave the way for the "new atheist" movement—a contemporary form of atheist apologetics popularized by Richard Dawkins, Daniel Dennett, Sam Harris, and Christopher Hitchens. Dawkins' *The God Delusion,* released in 2006, was a *New York Times* best seller and the second-best-selling book on Amazon that year. New atheism distinguishes itself from older forms of atheism in that it does not simply reject belief in God but also is hostile to those who hold religious views.

The term *secularism* was first coined by George Holyoake in the mid-nineteenth century in his work *Principles of Secularism.* Holyoake defined secularism in this way: "Secularism is a series of principles intended for the guidance of those who find theology indefinite, or inadequate, or deem it unreliable. It replaces theology, which mainly regards life as a sinful necessity, as a scene of tribulation through which we pass to a better world."[36]

While secularism spread through Europe in the eighteenth century, it took longer to take root in the United States, arriving in force in the late nineteenth and early twentieth centuries. In 1963, the Supreme Court ruled in *Abington School District v. Schempp* that school-sponsored Bible reading and prayer were unconstitutional. Madalyn Murray O'Hair, founder of American Atheists and the woman who brought a companion case, *Murray v. Curlett,* was an infamous leader in the push for the secularization of public schools in America.

Who are the key figures?

The four most famous proponents of atheism on the popular level today are Dawkins, Dennett, Harris, and Hitchens. While there are many other philosophers, scientists, academics, authors, politicians, entertainers, and activists who profess to be atheists or secularists, some of the more well-known proponents of atheism in recent years have been Stephen Hawking, the renowned theoretical physicist; Peter Singer, Ira W. DeCamp Professor of Bioethics at Princeton University; the best-selling novelist Philip Pullman; and Ray Kurzweil, noted inventor and advocate of transhumanism.

What are the main beliefs?

Atheism

I. **Denial of the existence of God.** Atheism is defined by the intellectual rejection of belief in the existence of gods in general and in a monotheistic God in particular. Many atheists differentiate between a positive atheism and a negative atheism. Positive atheism affirms the nonexistence of God. Negative atheism is the lack of belief in a particular God or gods. Negative atheism differs from the related idea of agnosticism, which holds that we do not know whether God exists. Some negative atheists acknowledge belief in the existence of supernatural beings while rejecting the idea of an ultimate self-existent supernatural being who made all things. Atheism is essentially the logical conclusion of materialism, the view that everything that exists is made up of physical matter.

II. **Materialistic theory of life.** Fundamental to all forms of atheism is the belief in a materialistic view of the world. Most evolutionary theories of origin are inexorably linked to an atheist philosophy. Though atheists offer a variety of explanations for the origin of the universe, all reject creationism. A materialistic view of the universe coincides with the atheistic rejection of an ordered purpose or transcendent ethic. Herman Bavinck explained, "Materialism asserts that there is no purpose in things, and the teleological [purposeful] interpretation of nature must give way to the mechanical [merely descriptive] one."[37] Whereas biblical Christianity teaches that there is a divinely intended purpose (teleology) to the created world, atheism rejects any need to structure reality according to a transcendent standard or to believe that there is an ultimate purpose to the universe. Atheists tend to acknowledge the need for societal ethics while rejecting the idea of an ethic based on a transcendent divine person and standard, namely, God and His eternal moral law.

Secularism

I. **No authority but human reason.** The chief principle of secularism is the belief in the autonomy of human reason, that is, human reason as the final standard in all things. Secularism is a fundamentally anti-revelatory religion. Adherents believe that they have everything necessary within themselves to accurately interpret and structure the world around them.

II. **Societal and political neutrality.** Secularism as a philosophy promotes the idea of state neutrality. Accordingly, the state must remain absolutely free from the influence of the church and from religion in general. Secularists reject the idea that the church or other religious institutions should be able to have any say in the state and its institutions.

Why do people believe this form of false teaching?

Fallen men and women seek absolute autonomy, that is, complete independence from God. The greatest expression of autonomy is freedom from the constraints of divine authority and governance. Atheism is the ultimate expression of philosophical detachment from the moral responsibility and culpability people have before their Creator. Secularism is the ultimate societal expression of liberation from divine government of men.

How does it hold up against biblical Christianity?

Atheism

I. **The self-existing God.** When God revealed Himself to Moses, He used the verb "I AM" (Ex. 3:14). The living and true God is that self-existent Being than which there is none greater. He is infinite, eternal, unchangeable, and self-sufficient in all His divine perfections. Through nature and the human conscience, God reveals Himself to all. As the Apostle Paul explained in Romans 1:20, God's "invisible attributes, namely, his eternal power and divine nature, have been clearly perceived, ever since the creation of the world, in the things that have been made." However, since people naturally exchange the truth of God for a lie (vv. 18, 25), no one can be saved through the general revelation of God in creation. Nevertheless, all people are daily confronted with the reality of being made in His image and living in the world He has created (Acts 17:25, 28).

II. **Creation and providence.** Scripture teaches that God spoke the world into existence by the word of His power in the space of six days (Gen. 1:1–31; Ps. 33:8–9; John 1:1–3; Heb. 11:3). When God revealed Himself to Job, He asked, "Where were you when I laid the foundation of the earth?" (Job 38:4). The self-sufficient and eternally existing triune God is before all things, and through Him all things have been made. Additionally, Scripture teaches that He upholds (sustains and guides) the universe "by the word of His power" (Heb. 1:3). God is guiding all the affairs of His creation to bring it to the end for which He has made it.

Secularism

I. **Supernatural special revelation.** From the beginning, man has needed God's special revelation—words that He speaks in addition to His revelation in the conscience and in nature—to properly interpret the world around him. When God gave Adam the command in the garden not to eat of the Tree of Knowledge of Good and Evil (Gen. 2:16–17), He was teaching Adam that he could not truly understand the general revelation of God apart from the special, spoken word of God. We also see this in the creation mandate that God gave to Adam and Eve when He created them: "Be fruitful and multiply and fill the earth and subdue it, and have dominion over the fish of the sea and over the birds of the heavens and over every living thing that moves on the earth" (1:28). If man needed God's special revelation at creation, how much more do we need it after the fall? We need God's special revelation not simply to enable us to understand His will and the meaning of the world around us but also to come to a saving knowledge of Him. Today, God's special revelation is contained in the Word of God inscripturated, the sixty-six books of the Old and New Testaments.

II. **No neutrality.** The Bible teaches that God is King over all the earth and that He reigns over the nations (Ps. 47:7–8). There is nothing in this world that remains untouched by His sovereign rule and dominion. God has created the world for Himself. Therefore, we are to do whatever we are engaged in to His glory (1 Cor. 10:31). While God has differentiated the spheres of His rule in this world (e.g., the church is not the state, and the state is not the church), He has not left any part of creation to be autonomously governed by men. The church is God's special manifestation of His kingly rule in the world, yet it is a leavening institution, intended by God to influence every aspect of society for His glory (Matt. 13:31–33).

How can I share the gospel with those who hold to this false teaching?

I. **Focus on the question of existence.** The question that we must present to an atheist or secularist is the question of existence: Why is there something rather than nothing? One who holds to a materialistic view of life cannot answer that question. He cannot answer why matter exists at all. All existence comes from the eternally self-existent God. Every effect must have a cause, and the universe is clearly an effect of some greater cause. Ultimately, there must be a first cause that set into motion other effects that themselves became causes of other effects, and so on. This first cause is the self-existent God, the One who has the power of being in Himself, the One who is self-existent and uncaused.

II. **Focus on issues of morality.** In an atheistic and secularist worldview, there can be no objective standard of reality. In Scripture, God has given us a transcendent ethic, which is summarily comprehended in the Ten Commandments. If men reject God's law as the transcendent ethic, binding on all people, there is no way for people to replace it with something else and have it be ultimately binding on themselves and the society around them. Seek opportunities with an atheist or secularist to discuss the need for a transcendent ethic. Explain that he cannot judge the ethics of another society or individual as wrong or evil unless he has an ethic that can judge both his own ethic and the ethics of others. Explain that the fact that he judges the ethics of others implies the existence of a normative standard outside himself to which he can appeal to evaluate others. There is a standard of good that he assumes and that all people, including himself, should be accountable to. That standard is God.

III. **Focus on reconciliation to God.** Our fundamental need is to be reconciled to God. All men need to be confronted with the truth about their fallen condition in Adam, their depraved sinful nature, and their need for an atoning sacrifice in order to be reconciled to the God they have rejected. All men are, by nature, atheistic in their hearts in the sense that they want nothing to do with the God who is. The psalmist said, "The fool says in his heart, 'There is no God'" (Ps. 14:1; 53:1). In Christ, God came into the world that He made in order to reveal Himself to men who have rejected Him because of their love of sin. On the cross, Jesus atoned for the sins of those who were once His enemies in order to bring them into a reconciled relationship with the triune God, and He was raised so that sinners can be declared righteous and receive the blessings of our Creator.

KEY DATE

—

1859

Eighteen fifty-nine saw the publication of *On the Origin of Species* by the English naturalist Charles Darwin. The book laid out Darwin's theories on the diversity of life, which he explained as owing to evolution by natural selection in a branching pattern from a common ancestor. This means that one species can produce numerous descendant species over the course of many generations through mutations that give it an advantage in its environment and which allow it to be more successful producing offspring. Darwin's theory was informed by research conducted during the voyage of the *HMS Beagle,* especially his observations of the finches of the Galapagos Islands. The book laid the groundwork for modern evolutionary biology but was immediately controversial, as it ran contrary to contemporary ideas about species' being fixed.

BERTRAND RUSSELL

▶ 1872–1970

Bertrand Russell, 3rd Earl Russell was a British philosopher, logician, mathematician, and writer. At age eighteen, Russell became an atheist after reading the autobiography of his godfather, John Stuart Mill, with its critique of the First Cause argument. Russell pursued a career in academia, which sometimes suffered because of his controversial views, his atheism, and his pacifism. He is considered one of the founders of analytic philosophy, which strove for clarity in philosophy after the work of David Hume, which Russell considered needlessly obscure. Among his notable works are *Principia Mathematica* and *A History of Philosophy*.

CONCLUSION

God changes hearts

God has not called His people to engage in apologetics merely to win arguments or debates. Rather, He calls Christians to defend and promote the Christian faith in order that through these efforts, God will win the souls of His elect to the Lord Jesus Christ. To that end, it is incumbent on us to study diligently the essential doctrines of the Christian faith in Scripture. As we study the biblical and historic teaching on essential Christian truths—and keep a watch over our lives—we will be better "prepared to make a defense to anyone who asks . . . with gentleness and respect, having a good conscience" (1 Peter 3:15–16).

Christians are to be zealous to spread the gospel to all those in this lost and perishing world.

Nevertheless, no amount of study or personal godliness can ever change another sinner's heart or give spiritual understanding of the truth of Scripture. By nature, all people are "dead in [their] trespasses and sins" (Eph. 2:1). Since the fall, all are "darkened in their understanding, alienated from the life of God because of the ignorance that is in them, due to their hardness of heart" (4:18). Nothing short of spiritual regeneration (i.e., new birth) will suffice to open the eyes of people's hearts and enable them to see and embrace the truth. Regeneration is the sovereign work of the Spirit of God. He alone can bring sinners from spiritual death to spiritual life. This is the clear teaching of Scripture. The Lord commanded the prophet Ezekiel to pray to the Spirit to come and give new life to dry bones in the valley (Ezek. 37:3–14). As Jesus told Nicodemus, "Unless one is born of water and the Spirit, he cannot enter the kingdom of God" (John 3:5).

In addition to regenerating sinners, the Holy Spirit alone can give spiritual illumination. Instead of giving new revelations, the Holy Spirit takes the revelation of Scripture and opens the minds and hearts of men to the truth about Christ. The Holy Spirit enables believers to see what God has clearly revealed in Scripture (Luke 24:27, 44). In his sermon "A Divine and Supernatural Light," Jonathan Edwards explained, "[The Holy Spirit] reveals no new doctrine . . . suggests no new proposition to the mind . . . teaches no new thing of God, or Christ, or another world, not taught in the Bible; but only gives a due apprehension of those things that are taught in the Word of God."[38]

The regenerating and illuminating work of the Holy Spirit is exemplified in Luke's account of the conversion of Lydia. Luke tells us that after Paul preached the gospel to a group of women in Philippi, "The Lord opened [Lydia's] heart to pay attention to what was said by Paul" (Acts 16:14). In his letter to the church in Ephesus, the Apostle Paul explained that he was praying that God would further enlighten the eyes of the hearts of believers so that they would be able to see all that they have in Christ (Eph. 1:18–20). The Puritan Thomas Manton summed up the necessity of the illuminating work of the Spirit when he wrote: "Without the assistance and counsel and illumination of the Holy Spirit we can do nothing in divine matters. . . . God's mind is revealed in Scripture, but we can see nothing without the spectacles of the Holy Spirit."[39]

Prayer and patience

Since it is entirely the work of God to set men free from the bondage of false teaching and religions, we must trust Him to do so for those with whom we share the gospel. We must fervently commit the salvation of our loved ones, neighbors, coworkers, and acquaintances to God in prayer. If the triune God alone can change the hearts of men, then we must rely on Him to do so. And we must be patient for the Lord to show His saving grace and mercy to those around us. When we remember how patient the Lord has been with us, how can we not be patient as we trust Him to change the hearts of others? Spiritual understanding and saving faith are based solely on the sovereign grace and mercy of God (Ex. 33:19; Rom. 9:15–16).

NOTES

1   Conrad Hackett and David McClendon, "Christians remain
     world's largest religious group but they are declining in Europe,"
     FactTank (blog), April 5, 2017, https://www.pewresearch.org
     /fact-tank/2017/04/05/christians-remain-worlds-largest
     -religious-group-but-they-are-declining-in-europe/.

2   Ligonier's 2018 State of Theology survey highlights the diversity
     of opinions about key biblical doctrines. You can find the results
     of the survey at https://thestateoftheology.com.

3   Christian Smith, "On 'Moralistic Therapeutic Deism' as U.S.
     Teenagers' Actual, Tacit, De Facto Religious Faith," Catholic
     Education Resource Center, accessed September 19, 2019,
     https://www.catholiceducation.org/en/controversy
     /common-misconceptions/on-moralistic-therapeutic-deism
     -as-u-s-teenagers-actual-tacit-de-facto-religious-faith.html.

4   Westminster Shorter Catechism 6.

5   Paragraph 2010 of the Catechism of the Catholic Church states,
     "Moved by the Holy Spirit and by charity, we can then merit for

ourselves and for others the graces needed for our sanctification, for the increase of grace and charity, and for the attainment of eternal life." Accessed September 9, 2019, http://www.vatican .va/archive/ENG0015/__P70.HTM.

6   For an explanation of the Marrow Controversy, see Sinclair Ferguson's Ligonier teaching series *The Whole Christ,* https://www .ligonier.org/learn/series/whole-christ.

7   Catechism of the Catholic Church, paragraphs 1266 and 2020, accessed September 9, 2019, http://www.vatican.va/archive /ENG0015/__P3N.HTM and http://www.vatican.va / archive/ENG0015/__P72.HTM.

8   "Facts and Statistics," The Church of Jesus Christ of Latter-day Saints, accessed February 20, 2020, https://newsroom .churchofjesuschrist.org/facts-and-statistics.

9   Most of this historical survey can be found in Joseph Smith—History from the Pearl of Great Price, accessed September 20, 2019, https://www.churchofjesuschrist.org/study/scriptures /pgp/js-h/1?lang=eng.

10   "Bible, Inerrancy of," The Church of Jesus Christ of Latter-day Saints, accessed September 20, 2019, https://www .churchofjesuschrist.org/study/manual/gospel-topics /bible-inerrancy-of?lang=eng.

11   Joseph Smith Jr., "The King Follett Sermon," The Church of Jesus Christ of Latter-day Saints, accessed April 20, 2020, https://www.churchofjesuschrist.org/study/ensign/1971/04 /the-king-follett-sermon?lang=eng.

12   Eliza R. Snow, *Biography and Family Record of Lorenzo Snow* (Salt Lake City: Deseret News, 1884), 46–47.

13   "Joseph Smith's Sermon on Plurality of Gods," Utah Lighthouse Ministry, accessed September 20, 2019, http://www.utlm.org /onlineresources/sermons_talks_interviews /smithpluralityofgodssermon.htm.

14   *Teachings of Presidents of the Church: Joseph F. Smith* (Salt Lake City: The Church of Jesus Christ of Latter-day Saints, 1998), 335.

15   Mary Baker Eddy, *Science and Health with a Key to the Scriptures* (Boston: Alison V. Stewart, 1918), 469.

16   Eddy, *Science and Health,* 256.

17   Eddy, *Science and Health,* 336–37.

18   Eddy, *Science and Health,* 470.

19   Eddy, *Science and Health,* 337.

20   Eddy, *Science and Health,* 447.

21   Eddy, *Science and Health,* 361.

22   Eddy, *Science and Health,* 25.

23   Eddy, *Science and Health,* 45–46.

24   Eddy, *Science and Health,* 18.

25   Mary Baker Eddy, "Message to the First Church of Christ, Scientist," in *Christian Science versus Pantheism* (Boston: Trustees under the Will of Mary Baker Eddy, June 15, 1902), 2.

26   "How Many Jehovah's Witnesses Are There Worldwide?" JW.org, accessed February 20, 2020, https://www.jw.org/en /jehovahs-witnesses/faq/how-many-jw/.

27 "The Global Religious Landscape," Pew Research Center,"
    accessed August 11, 2020, https://www.pewforum.
    org/2012/12/18/global-religious-landscape-exec/.

28 Conrad Hackett and Timmy Huynh, "What is each country's
    second largest religious group?" *Fact Tank* (blog), June 22,
    2015, accessed November 15, 2019, https://www
    .pewresearch.org/fact-tank/2015/06/22/what-is-each-countrys
    -second-largest-religious-group/.

29 Wendy Doniger, "Hindu Pluralism and Hindu Tolerance of the
    Other," in *Israel Oriental Studies XIV: Concept of the Other in
    Near Eastern Religions* (New York: E.J. Brill, 1994), 370.

30 Winfried Corduran, *Neighboring Faiths* (Downers Grove, Ill.:
    InterVarsity Press, 1998), 201.

31 Seth Govinda Das, *Hinduism,* cited by Paul Pathickal in *Christ and
    Hindu Diaspora* (Bloomington, Ind.: WestBow, 2012), 47–48.

32 One hundred years after Muhammed died, Ibn Ishaq—an
    eighth-century Arab author—wrote a biography of the proph-
    et's life titled *Sīrat Rasūl Allāh* (Life of the messenger of God).
    Although no original copy remains, an edited and revised ver-
    sion by Ibn Hisham, a ninth-century Arab scholar and author, is
    still in publication today.

33 The Quran, ed. Muhammad M. Pickthall (Medford, Mass.: Per-
    seus Digital Library, n.d.).

34 Jesse McKinley, "The Wisdom of the Ages, for Now Anyway,"
    The New York Times, March 23, 2008, accessed October 28,
    2019, https://nyti.ms/2q6AV94.

35 Herman Bavinck, *Reformed Dogmatics,* vol. 2, *God and Creation,* ed. John Bolt, trans. John Vriend (Grand Rapids, Mich.: Baker Academic, 2004), 343.

36 George Jacob Holyoake, *The Principles of Secularism* (London: 1871), https://www.gutenberg.org/files/36797/36797 -h/36797-h.htm.

37 Herman Bavinck, *Reformed Dogmatics*, vol. 2, *God and Creation*, ed. John Bolt, trans. John Vriend (Grand Rapids, Mich.: Baker Academic, 2004), 82.

38 Jonathan Edwards, "A Divine and Supernatural Light," in *The Works of Jonathan Edwards,* vol. 17, *Sermons and Discourses, 1730–1733,* eds. Mark Valeri and Harry S. Stout (New Haven, Conn.: Yale University Press, 1999), 412.

39 *The Complete Works of Thomas Manton* (London: Thomas Nisbet & Co., 1871), 4:307.

BIBLIOGRAPHY

Bavinck Herman. *Reformed Dogmatics,* vol. 2, *God and Creation.* Edited by John Bolt. Translated by John Vriend. Grand Rapids, Mich.: Baker Academic, 2004.

Belnap, Daniel J. "The King James Bible and the Book of Mormon," BYU Religious Study Center, https://rsc.byu.edu /archived/king-james-bible-and-restoration/10-king -james-bible-and-book-mormon.

Blomfield, Vishvapani. *Gautama Buddha: The Life and Teachings of The Awakened One.* London: Quercus, 2011.

Catechism of the Catholic Church. http://www.vatican.va/archive /ENG0015/__P70.HTM (accessed September 9, 2019).

Cosby, Brian. "Moralistic Therapeutic Deism: Not Just a Problem with Youth Ministry." The Gospel Coalition, April 9, 2012. https://www.thegospelcoalition.org/article /mtd-not-just-a-problem-with-youth-ministry/.

Chryssides, George W. "Defining the New Age." In *Handbook of the New Age*. Edited by Daren Kemp and James R. Lewis. Leiden, Netherlands: Brill, 2007.

Corduran, Winfried. *Neighboring Faiths*. Downers Grove, Ill.: Inter-Varsity Press, 1998.

Dalai Lama, XIV. *The Four Noble Truths: Fundamentals of the Buddhist Teaching*. London: Harper Collins Publishers, 1997.

Darwin, Charles. *The Origin of the Species by Natural Selection: or the Preservation of Favored Races in the Struggle for Life*. New York: D. Appleton and Co., 1882.

Duncan, J. Ligon. "God the Clockmaker." First Presbyterian Church, Jackson, Miss., June 9, 2014. https://www.fpcjackson.org /resource-library/sermons/what-in-the-world-is-this -world-thinking-god-the-clockmaker.

Eddy, Mary Baker. *The First Church of Christ Scientist and Miscellany*. Boston: Trustees Under the Will of Mary Baker Eddy, 1913.

———. *Science and Health with Key to the Scriptures*. Boston: Allison V. Stewart, 1918.

Esposito, John L. "Pillars of Islam." In *The Oxford Dictionary of Islam*, edited by John L. Esposito. Oxford, England: Oxford University Press, 2003.

Ferguson, Sinclair. *The Whole Christ: Legalism, Antinomianism, and Gospel Assurance; Why the Marrow Controversy Still Matters*. Wheaton, Ill.: Crossway, 2016.

Fisher, Edward. *The Marrow of Modern Divinity*. Fearn, Ross-shire, Scotland: Christian Heritage, 2009.

Frazier, Caroline. "Suffering Children and the Christian Science Church." *The Atlantic,* April, 1995. https://www.theatlantic.com/past/docs/unbound/flashbks/xsci/suffer.htm.

Gerstner, John H. *Teachings of Jehovah's Witnesses*. Grand Rapids, Mich.: Baker, 1983.

Hinn, Costi W. *God, Greed, and the (Prosperity) Gospel: How Truth Overwhelms a Life Built on Lies*. Grand Rapids, Mich.: Zondervan, 2019.

Hitchens, Christopher, Richard Dawkins, Sam Harris, and Daniel Dennett. *The Four Horsemen: The Conversation That Sparked an Atheist Revolution*. New York: Random House, 2019.

Hoekema, Anthony A. *Jehovah's Witnesses*. Grand Rapids, Mich.: Eerdmans, 1974.

Holyoake, George. *Principles of Secularization*. London: Austin and Co., 1871.

Hussain, Musharraf. *The Five Pillars of Islam: Laying the Foundations of Divine Love and Service to Humanity*. Leicestershire, England: Kube, 2012.

Johnson, Phil. "What's New with the New Age? Why Christians Need to Remain on Guard against the Threat of New Age Spirituality." In the *Southern Baptist Journal of Theology* 10 no. 4 (Winter 2006).

Kaiser, Walt. "The Old Testament Promise of Material Blessings and the Contemporary Believer." In *Trinity Journal* 9 no. 2 (Fall 1988).

The Koran. Translated from the Arabic by Rev. J.M. Rodwell. London: J.M. Dent and Sons, 1913.

Luther, Martin. "Against the Antinomians." In *Luther's Works,* vol. 47, *Christian in Society IV,* edited by Jaroslov Pelikan and Helmut T. Lehman. Philadelphia: Fortress, 1971.

Marx, Karl. *Das Kapital: A Critique of Political Economy.* Washington, D.C.: Regnery, 2012.

Miller, William. *A Christian's Response to Islam.* Phillipsburg, N.J.: P&R, 1976.

Morgan, Kenneth. *The Path of Buddha: Buddhism Interpreted by Buddhists.* New York: Motilal Banarsisass, 1956.

Narayanan, Vasudha. "Hinduism." In *Eastern Religions: Origins, Beliefs, Practices, Holy Texts, Sacred Places,* edited by Michael D. Coogan, Michael David Coogan, and Vasudha Narayanan. New York: Oxford University Press, 2005.

Nāṣirī, 'Alī. *An Introduction to Hadith: History and Sources.* London: MIU Press, 2013.

Paine, Thomas. *The Age of Reason: An Investigation of True and Fabulous Theology,* vol. 2. London: R. Carlisle, 1818.

Raymond, Erik. "The Soft Prosperity Gospel." In *Tabletalk,* April 1, 2016. https://www.ligonier.org/learn/articles/soft-prosperity-gospel/.

Russell, Bertrand. *Why I Am Not a Christian.* New York: Simon & Schuster, 1957.

Rig-Veda Sahnita: A Collection of Ancient Hindu Hymns. Translated by H.H. Wilson. London: William H. Allen and Co., 1857.

Smith, Christian. "On 'Moralistic Therapeutic Deism' as U.S. Teenagers' Actual, Tacit, De Facto Religious Faith." In *Princeton Lectures on Youth, Church, and Culture,* 2005. Princeton, N.J.: Princeton Theological Seminary, 2005.

Smith, Joseph. The Book of Mormon. Salt Lake City: The Church of Jesus Christ of Latter-day Saints, 2013.

———. The Doctrine and Covenants. Salt Lake City: The Church of Jesus Christ of Latter-day Saints, 2018.

———. The Pearl of Great Price. Salt Lake City: The Church of Jesus Christ of Latter-day Saints, 2018.

VanDoodewaard, William. *The Marrow Controversy and the Seceder Tradition.* Grand Rapids, Mich.: Reformation Heritage, 2011.

Vitello, Paul. "Christian Science Church Seeks Truce with Modern Medicine." *New York Times,* March 23, 2010. https://www.nytimes.com/2010/03/24/nyregion/24heal.html.

Quimby, Phineas P. *The Complete Collected Works of Dr. Phineas Parkhurst Quimby.* Belfast, Maine: Phineas Parkhurst Quimby Philosophical Society, 2008.

Zaka, Anees and Diane Coleman. *Truth about Islam: The Noble Qur'an's Teachings in Light of the Holy Bible.* Phillipsburg, N.J.: P&R, 2004.